THE HERMETIC RITE

ARYA AETERNA

Book III

THE HERMETIC RITE

Arya Aeterna Book III

Published by Sanctus Arya Press

First edition, published in April of 2026 by Sanctus Arya Press.

Paperback: 978-1-968394-04-2

Hardcover: 978-1-968394-05-9

Library of Congress Number pending.

Cover art, editing, and layout by Frater Sigma.

Inside illustrations taken from the public domain.

More at:

aryaaeterna.com

sanctusarya.com

This volume was crafted by anonymous initiates in service to the Great Work and furthering a Northern Esoteric Tradition of Perennial Wisdom.

Εἰ οὖν μὴ ἴσος τῷ θεῷ γένῃ, οὐ δύνασαι καταλαβεῖν τὸν θεόν· ὅμοιον γὰρ ὁμοίῳ γινώσκεται.

Ei oún mí ísos tó theó géni, ou dýnasai katalaveín tón theón: ómoion gár omoío ginósketai.

"If then you do not make yourself equal to God, you cannot apprehend God; for like is known by like."

— Corpus Hermeticum, Book XI

Table of Contents

Introduction

Across modernity's putrefying spiritual landscape, the "*man against time*" — a figure defined as one generally opposed to the degenerative currents of his era — faces a profound crisis. Contemporary "occulture" with its self-righteous debauchery, performative otherness, and petty resentments, has become a mire of malevolence and distraction. Far from offering a path to transcendence, it ensnares adherents in a cycle of egomania, indulgence, theatrics, and profanation.

Against this backdrop, a new magical system is required — one rejecting decadent tendencies and oriented toward an affirmation of the sacred. Stripped of its modern adulterants, Hermeticism stands as a potent framework for this purpose, providing a systematic means to surpass the profane and reclaim dominion.

Hermeticism in its authentic form is neither a relic of antiquarian curiosity, nor vehicle for self-indulgent play-acting and malicious depravity. It is a dynamic axis of vertical ascent connecting one though powerful practices to the metaphysical principles sustaining existence. Rooted in a synthesis of esoteric currents primarily from ancient Greece and Egypt, it offers an effective program of spiritual strength-training.

In *The Hermetic Tradition*, Julius Evola underscores its focus on operative transformation, where a practitioner engages with cosmic forces to refine their being. This is not a retreat into fantasy, but active confrontation — a process of aligning oneself with the infinite to overcome the desacralized nature of our modern world. Hermeticism demands intellectual rigor and practical discipline, fostering a state of inner supremacy that triumphs over the chaos of contemporary decay.

At the heart of this path lies the Rite as an initiatic technique aimed at apotheosis. Unlike devotional practices seeking external salvation, Hermetic techniques are liturgies designed to awaken higher consciousness and effect transformation. As Evola and his Ur Group verified, these rituals harness symbol, gesture, and intent to bridge immanent with transcendent.

The magus does not kneel in worship, but stands as an active participant employing visualization, meditation, and ritual acts to cultivate a direct experience of the divine. Distinct from religion, this process aligns with the Greek concept of *Henosis*: union with the Absolute, which one collaborates with in spiritual ascent. This Rite is a tool of self-mastery, transforming one into a vessel of ontological actuality.

Evola envisions an Absolute Individual as a being who has surpassed conditioned ego, achieving a state of pure autonomy and excellence. This ideal resonates deeply with Hermeticism's aim of realizing one's deific core, offering an updated articulation of its ancient goals. His emphasis on the sacred as an existing veracity (rather than intellectual conception) infuses Hermeticism with a profound vigor, compelling one to reject the purely theoretical.

An ultimate aim of the Hermetic path is actualization — a state where immanent and transcendent merge in a harmonious unity, summoning ancient Greek *Henosis*. This is a lived reality achieved through a structured initiatic methodology. One begins cultivating spiritual strength through rigorous self-discipline, employing rites to access higher planes of consciousness.

This process involves stripping away contingent layers of self — ego, desire, and material attachment — to reveal an unconditioned core of being. The result is a state of complete freedom where the individual stands as a sovereign entity, fully attuned with cosmic order. This actualization exceeds individual gratification, instead offering a profound sense of purpose: a restoration of the sacred in a world that has abandoned it.

Interpreted through an Evolian lens, Hermeticism offers a powerful antidote to the spiritual malaise of modernity. Far from the petty, aberrant, and contrived trappings of present-day "occulture," it stands as an organic convention rooted in a hallowed and methodical pursuit of apotheosis.

Through the Rite as an initiatic technique, a practitioner can forge a path to spiritual rule. The end goal — a realization of the Absolute Individual — merges immanence with transcendence, fulfilling the ancient promise of *Henosis*. In a world lost in the abyss, this path beckons as a return to the origin and call to reclaim a timeless grounding.

The Philosophy of Magic

From the perspective of Julius Evola, a prominent 20th-century Italian philosopher and esotericist, magic represents a disciplined path toward transcendence, aiming to align a practitioner with cosmic principles and realize the Absolute Individual, a state of complete spiritual autonomy. Drawing upon Evola's works such as *The Hermetic Tradition* and *Introduction to Magic*, as well as primary sources like the *Corpus Hermeticum* and *Greek Magical Papyri*, it is important we study the historical, philosophical, and cultural dimensions of magic from a Hermetic worldview.

Magic is a transformative art beyond simple manipulation of forces, and should instead stress spiritual ascent and realizing higher states of consciousness. Evola developed a doctrine of "magical idealism," which postulates mind as a primary reality, with the external world as a battleground between a subjective mental projection and potencies beyond one's control. The transmogrifying power of magic is one wherein a practitioner strives to transcend the mundane self and achieve metaphysical authority.

Unlike low magic, which pursues material outcomes such as wealth or influence, high magic (central to Evola's philosophy) seeks union with the divine and a refinement of consciousness. This aligns with a Hermetic principle of "as above, so below," suggesting the microcosm of an individual mirrors a universal macrocosm. It allows one to interface with forces eclipsing our ordinary power, which nevertheless may be found in ourselves.

Evola emphasized the true aim of magic is a "reconstruction of the integral man." A practitioner masters both their lower self and the forces of nature by embodying godlike principles. This is the fundamental premise underlying Hermeticism.

Evola's concept of the Absolute Individual is central to his philosophy of magic. Unlike modern individualism, which he critiqued as a cognitive error of regarding the phenomenal self — comprised of the five senses and discursive mind — as real, his is a supraindividual state connected to the transcendent and absolute often equated with divinity or the "*One*." In a Platonic cosmology influenced by thinkers like Alfarabi, Evola viewed the senses and egoic mind as variable and lacking substance, while Divine Intellect (*Nous*) and the One are supramundane and eternal.

Achieving this state requires extraordinary effort and rare gifts, as Evola noted in *Introduction to Magic, Vol. III*, where he described the Absolute Individual as an immortal and divine potential that magic seeks to realize. This pursuit is a rebellion against modern secular materialism, restoring one's connection to the Primordial Tradition.

The practice of magic involves three essential components: theoretical study, distinct preparation, and disciplined training. Theoretical study requires engaging with Hermetic texts such as the *Corpus Hermeticum*, which reveals the universe as a mental construct responsive to controlled will. These texts, attributed to

Hermes Trismegistus — a syncretic figure combining the Greek god Hermes and Egyptian Thoth — provide philosophical grounding for understanding the divine *Nous* as a source of all wisdom and the foundation of reality.

Functional preparation comprises meditation, visualization, and other techniques to strengthen spiritual energies. Ethical preparation encompasses cultivating virtues such as courage, detachment, and uprightness, ensuring the practitioner's purity and preventing corruption of spiritual power. The Baron's early experiments with magic, which he noted almost brought him to madness, underscore a need for such strictness to avoid psycho-spiritual harm.

Evola's philosophy of magic was shaped by his involvement with the *Gruppo di Ur*, a secret society he co-founded in 1927 with Arturo Reghini. The group aimed to explore and practice ancient rituals from Buddhist, Tantric, and Hermetic traditions to attain superhuman states of power and awareness. Their work, documented in the three-volume series *Introduction to Magic*, includes techniques for creating an etheric double, speaking words of power, using fragrances, interacting with entities, and forming a "magical chain."

These practices reflect Evola's belief in magic as a means to transcend the mundane and connect with higher realities, drawing from both Western and Eastern esoteric traditions. His correspondence with John Woodroffe, a scholar of Tantra, further deepened his interest in Eastern mysticism, particularly Tantra's active approach to spiritual experience.

Hermeticism began in Hellenistic Alexandria during the 2nd and 3rd centuries. Emerging in a cultural crossroads, it blended Greek philosophy (mainly Platonism and Stoicism) with Egyptian theological sciences and Near Eastern conjuring techniques. The *Corpus Hermeticum*, a compendium of texts ascribed to Hermes Trismegistus, encourages the soul's ascent to divine status and understanding, or *gnosis*, through practices such as meditation and ritual enactment.

Texts like *Poimandres* describe visions of the heavenly *Nous* shepherding a practitioner toward unity with the One: ultimate existence. *The Greek Magical Papyri* demonstrate Hermeticism's practical side, offering exercises to invoke deities like *Helios* for both spiritual and material intentions. While rooted in Greek ideas, this system incorporated Oriental elements, giving it a complex and somewhat cosmopolitan character.

Hermeticism was preserved in the Middle Ages by Arab and Byzantine scholars who translated and commented on its texts, ensuring their survival until the Renaissance. The 9th-century Arab intellectual Alfarabi amalgamated Hermetic conceptions with Neoplatonism, influencing later Islamic and Christian thinkers. In the Byzantine Empire, scholars like Michael Psellos studied Hermetic texts, contributing to their transmission to the West. This preservation laid the groundwork for a Renaissance revival, which marked a turning point in Hermeticism's history.

Hermeticism's resurgence was catalyzed by Marsilio Ficino's Latin translation of the *Corpus Hermeticum* commissioned by Cosimo de' Medici in 1463. Ficino, a Neoplatonist and priest, saw

Hermeticism as compatible with Christian theology and used it to support his philosophical and spiritual ideas. His translation made these ancient texts accessible to European intellectuals, sparking a renewed interest in Hermetic philosophy.

Ficino's approach emphasized Hermeticism's philosophical and spiritual dimensions, aligning it with a Neoplatonic focus on observation and ethical living. His Florentine Academy — a revival of Plato's Academy — became a center for studying Platonic and Hermetic thought, influencing the Renaissance's intellectual landscape. Ficino's *Platonic Theology* reflected a commitment to spiritual ascent with forthright applications.

In contrast, Giovanni Pico della Mirandola took a more varied approach. Mirandola in his *Oration on the Dignity of Man* (1486) proposed reconciling various philosophical and theological traditions including Hermeticism, Kabbalah, and Christianity. He believed all traditions contained fragments of a primordial wisdom that could be mingled to reveal hidden insight. Pico's *900 Theses*, intended for public debate in Florence, included propositions from Platonism, Aristotelianism, Hermeticism, and Kabbalah, reflecting his belief in the unity of all knowledge.

Although some theses were condemned by the Church as heretical, Pico's work laid a foundation for Christian Kabbalah, a significant change in Western esotericism. His multilingual education including Hebrew and Arabic enabled him to engage with Kabbalistic texts directly, adding Judaic terms, imagery, and religious practices into his philosophy. This syncretism also introduced an ornate ceremonial dimension to Hermeticism, diverging from Ficino's more austere and reflective emphasis.

The separation between Ficino's Platonic Hermeticism and Pico's Kabbalistic divergence shaped the trajectory of Western esotericism. Ficino's approach preserved an ontological consistency, preferring continuity over adaptation. Pico's syncretism, however, commenced subjecting it to eclectic customs blending Jewish, Chaldean, and other Near and Middle Eastern aspects, influencing later traditions like the Rosicrucians, founded in the early 17th century, and the Hermetic Order of the Golden Dawn, established in 1888.

These ostensibly Hermetic movements combined Kabbalistic, Gnostic, and increasingly Masonic elements, fabricating intricate symbolic and ceremonial systems. Additional Renaissance figures — such as Heinrich Cornelius Agrippa, whose *Three Books of Occult Philosophy* (1533) likewise established a system based in Hermetic, Kabbalistic, and Neoplatonic ideas, and also Giordano Bruno, who expanded Hermeticism into a pantheistic cosmology — diversified its purposes further. (Bruno's execution by the Inquisition in 1600 highlights the controversial nature of these ideas in a religious context.)

Evola critiqued the latter current as a dilution of Hermeticism's original clarity, arguing it echoed the excesses of late Greco-Roman sorcery, which he saw as contributing to cultural decline. He viewed the late Greco-Roman period as a time when spiritual practices devolved into superstition and materialism, a trend he believed was mirrored in what is now contemporary "Occulture."

This term, denoting a vulgarization and commodification of occult practices, includes movements like Theosophy (founded by Blavatsky in 1875), the Golden Dawn and its derivatives (especially Thelema), and New Age spirituality as a whole. Evola saw these as degenerative, prioritizing embellishment, influence, and material benefit over authentic transcendence. For example, Blavatsky's uncommon approach to esotericism initially emphasized psychic spectacles over metaphysical profundity, while the Golden Dawn's ostentatious practices (though rooted in Hermeticism) drew upon shadowy communiques from their enigmatic "Secret Chiefs."

Evola's counter-current sought to restore Hermeticism to its Greco-Egyptian roots, highlighting Platonic and Indo-European elements over Kabbalistic influences. He argued that Kabbalah's emphasis on representational systems (such as the *Sephirot*) and procedural observances ensnared seekers in sophisticated novelty, contrary to the Platonic focus on pure spiritual ascent.

His Aryo-Hermetic approach draws principally from Greek philosophy and emphasizes spiritual rigor, heroic virtue, and an experiential view of the cosmos. Evola saw these as expressions of a primal wisdom and universal truth underlying all genuine paths. For instance, the warrior ethos of Greek mythology, as perceived in figures like Achilles, echoes an ideal of self-mastery he esteemed.

Evola's philosophy of magic reflects his broader worldview, which was aristocratic, aggressive, and anti-egalitarian. He saw magic as a tool of an elite capable of transcending the mundane. His ideological association underscores a belief in spiritual hierarchy and demand for returning to traditional principles.

In *Revolt Against the Modern World*, Evola argued that modern civilization had lost its connection to the sacred — and magic offered a path to restore this link. His critique was not merely philosophical but cultural, seeing mainstream spirituality as symptomatic of a broader societal decline.

In its original, aristocratic form, Hermeticism offers a valuable structure for spiritual greatness, emphasizing high magic as a path to the Absolute Individual. This approach draws on Greco-Egyptian traditions while rejecting the syncretic confusion and decadent excess of modern "Occulture."

From its Alexandrian origins to its Renaissance revival, the historical evolution of Hermeticism reveals a tension between integrity and erosion shaping Western Esotericism's trajectory. Evola's Aryo-Hermetic counter-current based in Indo-European spirituality seeks to restore Hermeticism's focus on spiritual ascent, countering a decadence of contemporary esoteric practices. By highlighting discipline, examination, and heroic values, Evolian Hermeticism provides a challenging yet operational model for those seeking an actualized spiritual existence in the modern world.

Alchemical Symbolism and the Great Work

Far more than a mere precursor to chemistry, alchemy is a sacred science of spiritual transformation. Julius Evola's work *The Hermetic Tradition* interprets the alchemical process as a path to transcend the human condition, achieving what he calls the Absolute Individual — a state of sacred autonomy. The Great Work (or *Magnum Opus*) is a transformational journey seeking the "Philosopher's Stone," symbolizing a perfected self.

This process advances through stages — *Nigredo*, *Albedo*, *Citrinitas*, and *Rubedo* — each marked by profound symbolic meaning. Accompanying these phases are fundamental symbols such as the four elements, three primes, seven metals/planets, and Philosopher's Stone, serving as guides for a practitioner's inner work. Through functional contemplation, these symbols become tools for transmutation, allying an individual with primordial principles and a transcendent order.

The alchemical process is a structured journey with each stage representing a segment of spiritual development. Evola emphasizes these phases are metaphysical, reflecting changes in consciousness and being.

Nigredo: The black stage initiates the Great Work, symbolizing dissolution and confrontation with the shadow self. It is a period of chaos where ego and material attachments are broken down, akin to a symbolic death. This stage prepares a practitioner for rebirth by clearing impurities.

Albedo: The white stage follows, representing purification and illumination. Here a practitioner achieves clarity as the soul is cleansed and allied with superior principles. Symbolized by the Moon and Silver, *Albedo* marks an emergence of a luminous, spiritual state.

Citrinitas: Overlooked in some traditions, this yellow stage signifies awakening of transcendent insight. Associated with the element of air and enlightenment, it bridges the purity of *Albedo* with the perfection of *Rubedo*, fostering a deeper understanding of sacred reality.

Rubedo: The red stage is the zenith where one accomplishes integration and holy perfection. *Rubedo* represents a formation of the Philosopher's Stone, embodying an Absolute Individual's unity with the divine.

Alchemical symbols are not simple metaphors, but active tools encoding ontological realities. They guide a practitioner by connecting microcosm (self) with macrocosm (God).

Four Elements: Fire, Water, Air, and Earth, often depicted as a cross, represent foundational aspects of existence. Fire (active, transformative) corresponds to north/above, water (receptive, fluid) to the south/beneath, air (intellectual, communicative) to east/right, and earth (stable, material) to west/left. Balancing these elements within oneself is crucial for harmony.

Three Primes: Sulfur (soul, sentience), Mercury (spirit, vigor), and Salt (body, matter) are essential aspects of being. Their purification and union are foremost in the alchemical process, transforming a practitioner's inner nature.

Seven Metals/Planets: Each metal corresponds to a planet and quality: Gold/Sun (superiority), Silver/Moon (perception), Quicksilver/Mercury (volatility), Copper/Venus (compassion), Iron/Mars (strength), Tin/Jupiter (expansion), and Lead/Saturn (limitation). These characterize aspects of self that must be transmuted.

Philosopher's Stone: The ultimate symbol of the Great Work, it represents spiritual illumination, immortality, and a perfected self capable of transforming base elements into divine essence.

Active contemplation of alchemical symbols and stages is a powerful method for inner transmutation. By meditating on these representations, a practitioner assumes their meanings, linking their consciousness with celestial forces. For example, visualizing the *Nigredo* stage as a dark void can help confront fears, while focusing on the Philosopher's Stone inspires a pursuit of spiritual perfection. These practices, established as Evola's "Royal Art" (*Ars Regia*), empower one to deliberately shape their spiritual destiny.

Let us expound on this critical conceptual framework. Alchemy is a sacred discipline surpassing material science, aiding on a path of self-transformation and realization of the Absolute Individual. In

The Hermetic Tradition, Evola presents it as the *Ars Regia* — a heroic and initiatic process aimed at reintegrating the practitioner with a primordial, divine state.

Nigredo, or the black stage, initiates the Great Work with dissolution and decomposition. Evola describes it as a state of "alchemical death" or "blacker than black," where a practitioner confronts the chaos of their psyche, dismantling their ego and attachments. Symbolized by the planet Saturn and images like a raven or the tomb of Osiris, *Nigredo* represents a crisis where vital forces no longer hold an organism together.

This is fraught with risk; one must navigate the "trial of the void," preserving a "quintessence" amidst destruction. *Nigredo* involves facing one's shadow — subconscious fears, desires, and limitations — to clear a way for renewal. The phase corresponds to initiatory rites of death and renewal across ancient traditions.

Albedo produces cleansing illumination. This stage, associated with the color white and the Moon, marks an emergence of a luminous spiritual state. Evola describes *Albedo* as the "White Stone" or Silver, symbolizing an early embodiment of spirit. One achieves lucidity as a soul is refined through processes like washing and distillation, which separate the pure from impure.

Symbolically, *Albedo* is linked with the feminine principle, element of water, and figures like Diana, representing purity and rebirth. Mircea Eliade connects this stage to an alchemist's quest for a "new body" free of the terrestrial. For the practitioner, *Albedo* is a time of introspection, cultivating virtues like patience and humility to prepare for higher stages.

Citrinitas represents an awakening of spiritual insight and intellectual illumination. Though less emphasized, it is a known phase in traditional alchemy. Signified by the color yellow and associated with the element of air, *Citrinitas* implies a dawn of true understanding.

Here the practitioner begins to perceive divine reality. This stage involves integrating purified elements, fostering a deeper connection to the godhead and sacred order. Eliade suggests that *Citrinitas* reflects an alchemist's growing awareness of the unity between microcosm and macrocosm. This phase is correlated with a development of higher consciousness, preparing one for the final transformation.

Rubedo, the red stage, is a decisive culmination of the Great Work when one achieves excellence and integration. Signified by the color red, *Rubedo* represents a creation of the Philosopher's Stone and realization of the Absolute Individual. Evola describes this stage as the "Red Work," where the masculine (Sun/Sulfur) dominates and absorbs the feminine (Moon/Mercury), achieving a "supercosmic" immortality.

The procedure of coagulation stabilizes volatile elements, merging body, spirit, and soul. Eliade emphasizes that *Rubedo* signifies an alchemist's mastery over nature, personifying divine power. This stage is an ultimate objective where one becomes a sovereign being fully aligned with the eternal.

Alchemical symbols are not abstractions, but active tools encoding metaphysical realities while guiding a practitioner through the Great Work. Evola's *Hermetic Tradition* and Eliade's

Forge and Crucible provide a rich framework for understanding these symbols.

The four elements — Fire, Water, Air, and Earth — are foundational to Hermetic cosmology, represented by a cross symbolizing their unity and opposition. Evola describes them as states of understanding and corporeal manifestation. Fire (north/above) is active and transformative, driving purification. Water (south/below) is receptive and fluid, linked to dissolution. Air (east/right) is intellectual and communicative, fostering insight. Earth (west/left) is stable and material, grounding the process. Balancing the elements within oneself is essential for spiritual congruence. This mimics a fundamental Hermetic correspondence of microcosm-macrocosm.

The three primes — Sulfur, Mercury, and Salt — represent the essential components of being. Associated with the soul and fire, Sulfur embodies an active, masculine principle of will and individuation. Linked to spirit and water, Mercury is a vehicle of modification: fluid and dual-natured, capable of dissolving and transfiguring. Tied to the body and earth, Salt denotes stability and limitation, requiring purification to unlock its potential. The process involves purifying and uniting these primes to achieve a harmonious whole, as Eliade notes in a context of synthesis.

Each related to a planet, the metals symbolize qualities. Their correspondences: Gold/Sun (nobleness and virtuosity), Silver/Moon (perception and receptivity), Quicksilver/Mercury (fluidity and transformation), Copper/Venus (compassion and accord), Iron/Mars (strength and vigor), Tin/Jupiter (expansion, growth), and Lead/Saturn (limitation and matter).

From the heavy, terrestrial Lead to radiant, divine Gold, each metal represents an aspect of self that must be metamorphosed. Eliade connects these correspondences to ancient metallurgical rituals in which metals were perceived as living entities.

The Philosopher's Stone is an ultimate symbol of the Great Work representing spiritual enlightenment, immortality, and a refined self. Evola describes it as an occult principle acquired through "intelligence, inspiration, or divine revelation," not a physical object. It symbolizes an Absolute Individual capable of transmuting base elements into divine essence. Eliade views it as a culmination of an alchemist's quest for mastery over matter and spirit. The Stone is both a goal and tool, embodying a unity of alchemical processes.

The Royal Art emphasizes active engagement with alchemical symbols to effect inner transmutation. Active contemplation involves meditating on symbols to internalize their meanings and catalyze spiritual change. This practice aligns with Evola's Magical Idealism, wherein the mind shapes reality through focused intent.

This exercise balances the elements within a practitioner. Sit in a quiet space and close your eyes. Visualize a cross, with each arm representing an element: Fire (top), Air (right), Water (bottom), Earth (left). Focus on each element, reflecting on its qualities. Center your focus on the cross's midpoint: the Quintessence, symbolizing unity. Hold this image, integrating the elements within your being.

Alchemical symbolism offers an insightful basis for spiritual transformation. The stages of *Nigredo*, *Albedo*, *Citrinitas*, and *Rubedo* guide one through a journey of dissolution, purification, insight, and integration, culminating in the realization of the Absolute Individual. Symbols like the four elements, three primes, seven metals/planets, and Philosopher's Stone encode metaphysical truths, serving as tools for active contemplation.

By meditating upon these sacred symbols a practitioner can internalize their significance, linking with cosmic instruction and effecting an inner transmutation. While Evola's esoteric elitism may be controversial, his approach provides a disciplined path for those seeking to transcend the nadir of profane modernity and achieve spiritual dominion.

The Absolute Individual

The Absolute Individual emerges in Julius Evola's esoteric philosophy as an ultimate example of human potential: a being who transcends egoic limits and the material world's conditions to achieve holy reign. This notion captures a state of being wherein one becomes a self-sufficient, unconditioned center of power and ontological vigor. Central to this vision is deification: a process of "becoming God" — the apex of esoteric endeavors.

The Absolute Individual as articulated by Evola is not a mere enhancement of a personal self, but an essential transcendence of it. In *Theory of the Absolute Individual*, he describes this state as a return to a primordial, unconditioned existence where an individual is no longer shaped by external forces — social, psychological, or material — but instead embodies a sovereign essence.

This sovereignty is spiritual rather than political, reflecting Evola's broader metaphysical framework of Radical Tradition which envisions primeval sacred order as an ideal. The Absolute Individual thus stands as a microcosmic reflection of divinity, free from the contingencies of modernity and rooted in eternal values.

Unlike the fragmented and ego-driven self of contemporary society, an Absolute Individual achieves a unity of being that integrates body, mind, and spirit into a harmonious whole. This is not passive, but requires active effort — a deliberate rejection of the profane and reclamation of one's divine inheritance. For Evola, this is the true meaning of individuality: not isolation, but a state of completeness mirroring the Absolute itself.

Deification stands at the center of esotericism, representing a transformation of human into divinity. This is an incorporeal shift wherein a practitioner realizes their fundamental identity with otherworldliness. In Hermetic writings this aspiration is vividly expressed:

Εἰ οὖν μὴ ἴσος τῷ θεῷ γένῃ, οὐ δύνασαι καταλαβεῖν τὸν θεόν· ὅμοιον γὰρ ὁμοίῳ γινώσκεται.

Ei oún mí ísos tó theó géni, ou dýnasai katalaveín tón theón: ómoion gár omoío ginósketai.

"If then you do not make yourself equal to God, you cannot apprehend God; for like is known by like."

—Corpus Hermeticum, Book XI

This passage highlights the view that human beings possess a latent capacity to ascend to divinity. It is a process requiring both understanding (*gnosis*) and transformation (*praxis*). Evola adopts this belief, interpreting it as a call to surpass the human condition and regain a deific chrism lost to present-day degeneracy.

Comparatively, in Hinduism the concept of *moksha* parallels this aim. Liberation involves dissolving the ego and recognizing one's unity with *Brahman*, the ultimate reality. It is a procedure analogous to self-deification.

In *Taoism: The Magic, the Mysticism*, Evola explores the Taoist pursuit of *Tao* (the way), where practices like *wu wei* (non-action) align an individual with cosmic order, yielding a state of near-divine harmony. While distinct, these traditions share a common thread: an elevation of self beyond the commonplace through disciplined effort. This is a theme Evola adapts to his esoteric elitism.

Attaining the state of an Absolute Individual demands a rigorous journey of self-mastery and ritual praxis. It is a process Evola equates to transmutation. Drawing from *The Hermetic Tradition*, he frames this progression in alchemical terms with phases signifying one's spiritual ascent:

Nigredo is the initial dissolution wherein one confronts and dismantles their ego, purging attachments and illusions. This stage represents a necessary breakdown of the conditioned self, clearing a way for spiritual rebirth.

Albedo is a phase of purification, refining the soul through discipline and affiliating it with higher principles. This is when a practitioner cultivates clarity and detachment, washing away impurities to reveal the soul's latent potential.

Citrinitas is an awakening of the inner light where a purified soul begins to radiate spiritual illumination. This stage marks a dawn of true spiritual insight as a practitioner starts to perceive the divine within. It prepares an individual for the final step of divine union.

Rubedo is the culminating unification where an individual merges with the divine, achieving spiritual sovereignty. In this stage one realizes their essential identity with god, completing the transformation into an Absolute Individual.

This journey is not intellectual but experiential, requiring a practitioner to engage in rituals and exercises that reshape their being. The Ur Group's *Introduction to Magic* series emphasizes the operative nature of this path, offering techniques to awaken latent faculties and transcend ordinary consciousness. For Evola this became a solitary endeavor reserved for those with the will to undertake such a transformative path.

Hermeticism serves as an ideal means for self-deification, blending philosophical insight with practical techniques. The *Corpus Hermeticum* posits that, as microcosms of divine reality, humans can ascend through the spheres to reunite with Source — a state exemplified in Evola's Absolute Individual. In *The Hermetic Tradition* he explores alchemical symbolism as a guide for this ascent, viewing it as a primarily inner spiritual practice rather than an external and material one.

The Ur Group's *Introduction to Magic* complements this by offering rituals, meditations, and exercises to facilitate spiritual transformation. Ranging from visualizations to invocations, these practices aim to facilitate ontological awareness, making Hermeticism a bridge between theory and practice.

An initial set of standards is essential for those beginning their journey toward the Absolute Individual. Approach the path with a genuine desire for spiritual elevation, free from egoistic aims.

Maintain a consistent practice schedule, cultivating an unwavering will. Release material attachments, fostering inner independence. Uphold a personal code of honor, avoiding actions that compromise spiritual progress. These establish a groundwork for deeper esoteric work requiring dedication and consistency to yield results.

The Absolute Individual stands an archetype of mankind's highest potential: a sovereign being who through deification transcends the ego and aligns with the divine. Confirmed in parallel traditions like Hinduism and Taoism, this aspiration demands a disciplined journey of self-mastery and ritual praxis.

By leveraging Hermetic values and exercises, a practitioner can begin reclaiming a spiritual authority that defies the modern world's limitations. The Absolute Individual is not a distant ideal, but a living possibility for those willing to embrace its rigorous demands.

The Great Triad

Guénon's *The Great Triad* presents a metaphysical model centered on the ternary of Heaven, Man, and Earth, which he sees as a primary structure across spiritual traditions. Heaven denotes Essence, the unmanifest source of being; Earth signifies Substance, the discernable world of form; and Man acts as the mediator, harmonizing these realms. This framework parallels alchemical principles, where transformation involves balancing spiritual and material forces.

For instance, "*Solve et Coagula*" (dissolve and coagulate) symbolizes the elimination of impurities and reintegration into a higher state, mirroring the relationship of Heaven and Earth. Similarly, "*Animus, Spiritus, Corpus*" (Soul, Spirit, Body) and "Sulphur, Mercury, Salt" reflect this same triadic structure, with Soul/Sulphur as an active divine principle, Spirit/Mercury as transformative intermediary, and Body/Salt as a material basis. Guénon roots these concepts in Taoist cosmology, particularly Yin (Earth) and Yang (Heaven), with Man as the balancing force.

Evola's *Taoism: The Magic, the Mysticism* interprets Taoism as a metaphysical path to transcendence, emphasizing the Tao as an ultimate, invariable principle. Unlike Guénon's theoretical focus, Evola highlights applied skills — meditation, breathwork, and alchemy — to achieve detachment and divine rulership.

This state, akin to a Taoist "Immortal," transcends ego and societal constraints, uniting with the godhead. Evola associates Taoism to Hermeticism, both stressing esoteric transformation over religious devoutness, and rejects purely theistic frameworks like Christianity for their lack of initiatory depth.

Integrating Guénon's abstract insights with Evola's practical methodology offers a robust conduit to the Absolute Individual. Practitioners can use alchemical representations to guide inner transformation, reflecting upon "*Solve et Coagula*" to dissolve egoic attachments and incorporate refined properties. Techniques like meditation and ritual encourage self-control and alignment with transcendent potencies, facilitating the comprehension of spiritual sovereignty.

From an Evolian perspective, René Guénon's *The Great Triad* provides a metaphysical framework that illuminates universal principles governing spiritual transformation — particularly via alchemical conceptions like "*Solve et Coagula.*" In *Triad*, Guénon articulates a universal metaphysical structure centered on the ternary of Heaven, Man, and Earth, which he sees as an essential pattern across spiritual traditions.

Heaven characterizes Essence, an unmanifest source of all. Earth indicates Substance, the evident world of form and matter. As mediator, man performs a *"pontifex"* function of uniting these realms, sacralizing matter whilst grounding divinity. This triadic structure reflects Hermetic principles, providing a framework for understanding.

Solve et Coagula: This alchemical maxim, meaning "dissolve and coagulate," encapsulates dual processes of dissolution and reintegration. "Solve" infers Heaven's expansive, sacralizing effect, eliminating impurities and attachments. "Coagula" connects to Earth's obstructive, materializing force, consolidating purified elements into a higher state. Guénon sees this as a comprehensive principle reflected in Taoist Yin-Yang dynamics where an interplay of opposites initiates cosmic and individual transformation.

Animus, Spiritus, Corpus: This ternary signifies the psychic, spiritual, and physical dimensions of being. *Animus* (Soul) links to Heaven, divine substance; *Spiritus* (Spirit) to Man, a reconciling principle; and *Corpus* (Body) to Earth, material form. These must be purified and unified to reach ontological accord via a process of alchemical transmutation.

Sulphur, Mercury, Salt: The three primes symbolize active, transformative, and stabilizing principles. Sulphur, associated with soul, embodies an active, aware presence; Mercury, linked to spirit, represents a mutable vitality; and Salt, tied to the body, provides form and temporality. Guénon associates these with a "Great Triad" wherein Sulphur reflects Heaven's consciousness, Mercury Man's mediation, and Salt Earth's solidity.

In *The Great Triad*, Guénon roots these alchemical concepts in Taoist cosmology, particularly an interplay of Yin and Yang. Yang, associated with Heaven, is active and transcendent, while Yin, linked to Earth, is passive and physical. The Double Spiral, a Taoist symbol, illustrates their cyclical interaction, mirroring "*Solve et Coagula.*"

Man, as a "Son of Heaven and Earth," equalizes these forces, embodying the *Tao* — an ultimate unity underlying all existence. Guénon's approach also emphasizes the universal applicability of these principles across traditions.

In *Taoism: The Magic, the Mysticism*, Julius Evola presents Taoism as a metaphysical doctrine focused on direct experience of the *Tao*, an unchanging principle governing all existence. Unlike Guénon's broad metaphysical analysis, Evola highlights Taoism's practical and initiatory aspects, aligning it with his concept of an Absolute Individual — a being who achieves sacred authority.

Evola describes Tao as a transcendent reality symbolized as the "one of Heaven" or "bottom of a great valley," contrasting with a flux of mundane existence. The Taoist concept of immortality involves a "de-coagulation" of form, achieving an association with a fixed Principle akin to the Absolute Individual.

Operative Taoist exercises — involving meditation, breathwork, alchemy, and qigong — are aimed at accomplishing detachment and restoring the "throne of the One." These techniques cultivate "active immobility," a state of balanced neutrality free from desire or a need for moralism.

An initiatory hierarchy — *long-sang*, *phiracy*, and *hub* — guides practitioners toward becoming an "Immortal," a figure indifferent, yet exceedingly formidable. These practices are highly comparable to Hermeticism and its associated schools, observing their mutual emphasis on esoteric transformation.

One commences by understanding the Great Triad's structure: Heaven (Animus/Sulphur), Man (Spiritus/Mercury), and Earth (Corpus/Salt). This parallels the Hermetic microcosm-macrocosm correspondence where an individual reflects the cosmos. "*Solve et Coagula*" guides the process: dissolving ego attachments and reintegrating purified aspects into a unified whole. The three primes — Sulphur (active awareness), Mercury (transformative lifeforce), and Salt (firm structure) — must be balanced to achieve harmony.

Again, the goal is to transcend ego limitations, achieving a state of spiritual sovereignty analogous to Evola's Absolute Individual or a Taoist "Immortal." Through meticulous preparation, one dissolves mundane attachments (Solve) and reintegrates as a unified, divine being (Coagula), culminating in *Henosis*.

Hermetic Cosmology

The Hermetic cosmos is a profound metaphysical framework of a living, systematic totality suffused with divine significance. This idea, established in the *Corpus Hermeticum*, posits a fundamental correspondence between the microcosm of a human and macrocosm of the universe.

This is a principle encapsulated in the axiom "*Tò ἄνω θάτερον τοῦ κάτωθεν, καὶ τὸ κάτωθεν θάτερον τοῦ ἄνωθεν*" ("That which is above is like that which is below, and that which is below is like that which is above"). Here, mankind emerges as a reflection of the heavenly order, comprising a tripartite arrangement — soul (***Nous,*** "**Νοῦς**"), spirit (***Pneuma,*** "**Πνεῦμα**"), and body (***Soma,*** "**Σῶμα**") — which mirrors the cosmos's own division into mental, etheric, and material realms.

As the principle of pure awareness, *Nous* corresponds to the divine realm, source of pure archetypes and emanative intellect; *Pneuma*, exciting breath or spirit, aligns with the etheric realm, plane of vigor and refined form; and *Soma*, the corporeal vessel, reflects a solid realm of tangible expression. This is an effective alchemical process of self-transformation wherein knowledge (*gnosis*) and disciplined practice elevate an individual toward the Absolute, realizing their latent divinity.

The planets in Hermeticism and alchemy assume a pivotal role as dynamic agents within this cosmology, far transcending their astronomical identities to become symbols of spiritual forces and stages of transformation. Each planet exerts an astrological potency, shaping the human psyche and alchemical work through its unique influence. As the *Corpus Hermeticum* declares, "**Επτὰ δὲ πλανητῶν χοροὶ τὸν κόσμον περιέχουσι**" ("Seven planetary choirs encompass the cosmos"), suggesting these celestial spheres form a hierarchical ladder through which a soul navigates its incarnatory descent and potential return. Linked to lead, Saturn characterizes the *Prima Materia* — an unrefined foundation of being — while the Sun, associated with gold, signifies a perfected state of enlightenment.

These planetary influences serve as manifestation conditioners, imprinting qualities upon the soul as it enters the material plane and offering pathways for its liberation during ascent. In Evola's *The Hermetic Tradition*, this process is framed as an experiential clash with these archetypal forces where one must transfigure inner planetary correspondences (overcoming Saturn's inertia or harnessing Jupiter's expansive nobility) to accomplish godlike autonomy. Accordingly, the alchemical journey mirrors a planetary interplay with each step, refining the microcosm in relation with a macrocosmic order and reflecting a divine harmony underlying all existence.

In the Indo-European tradition, the "Cosmic Man" appears as a strong emblem of this celestial unity, personifying a primordial archetype from which the universe itself is fashioned. Figures such as Proto-Indo-European **Yemo*, Greek *Phanes*, and Vedic *Purusha* illustrate this concept across cultures. In the *Rigveda*, *Purusha's* sacrifice is the generative act of creation: "**पुरुष एवेदं सर्वं यद्भूतं यच्च भव्यम्**" ("*Purusha is all that has been and all that will be*"), his dismembered body giving rise to the planes of reality.

Associated with fire, the Divine Plane constitutes the highest realm of pure spirit and divine archetypes, akin to the World of Emanation where the essence of the Cosmic Man originates. This is a domain of unmanifest potential and the eternal source from which all lower planes emanate.

The Astral Plane, linked to air, serves as a creative realm of idea and image. Here, inspiration shapes concepts and systems, reflecting *Purusha's* consciousness dispersed into the cosmos.

Linked to water, the Ethereal Plane acts as a formative layer. It is a subtle vigor supporting and animating the physical world, connecting matter to superior dimensions, like a spectral mirror of physical countenance.

Finally, the Material Plane, grounded in earth, is a sphere of manifestation where the elements coalesce into palpable reality, embodying the perceptible remnants of Cosmic Man's sacrifice.

This dismemberment may be seen as a representation for the fragmentation of self in a material world, with the alchemical work aiming to reintegrate these planes within a practitioner, restoring a primordial wholeness of an Absolute Individual. The four planes of reality are dynamic stages of transformation, each demanding a specific engagement from an inductee.

In the Material Plane, this method begins with a process of *Putrefactio* (putrefaction), where the *Soma* undergoes a necessary decay to break down old structures and release the vital essence hidden within. This grounded realm, rich with earthly density, sets a foundation for ascent by composting the remnants of mundane existence.

The Ethereal Plane follows, wherein the changeable *Pneuma* engages in *Sublimatio* (sublimation), refining a soul through fluid dissolution and elevation, carrying it skyward like vapor toward higher realms. This is the domain of dynamic changeability — a bridge between the physical and the subtle.

With its airy structure, the Astral Plane enables *Fermentatio* (fermentation), transforming refined essence into a potent vitality through meditative insight and alignment with divine archetypes. Here, the *Logos's* perspicuity allows one to encompass purpose and intelligence, mirroring the creative order of a greater mind.

This stage prepares the initiate for a final unification in the Divine Plane, where *Proiectio* (projection) solidifies the perfected essence into transcendent expression, with the Nous now a radiant vessel embodying divine order.

Evola emphasizes the recurrent nature of this process, a repeated refinement akin to the planetary orbits, culminating in the Philosopher's Stone. It is a symbol of a reconstituted Cosmic Man, balancing all planes into a singular, transcendent reality.

This universe extends beyond abstract constructs to engage one in a lived, experiential relationship with the deific order. The *Greek*

Magical Papyri offer practices to activate this process, like invocations to planetary divinities to align one's faculties with macrocosmic energies. These practices are not ordinary rituals, but transformative acts that awaken a latent godhood within.

The *Nous*, as a spark of divine intellect, is cultivated through meditative focus on the infinite, often denoted by an alchemical Sun, which burns away veils of illusion to reveal an unmanifest truth. *Pneuma*, as vital breath, is refined through breathwork and visualization, aligning with a fluid Etheric Plane to channel nascent energies. Rooted in matter, the *Soma* is purified through disciplined asceticism, transforming the body into a temple of the divine, as seen in the maxim "*transmutamini de lapidibus mortuis in vivos lapides philosophicos*" ("be transmuted from dead stones into living philosophical stones").

This process reflects the Indo-European motif of the Cosmic Man's reintegration. Here a fragmented self is reconstituted through heroic effort. This echoes the Norse myth of *Ymir*, whose body forms the world and essence can be reclaimed by an initiate.

The planetary hierarchy further enriches this cosmology by assigning specific roles to each celestial body in the alchemical work. In Evola's framework the Moon, associated with silver, governs the Ethereal Plane's fluid vitality, mediating specifically the material and astral. Venus, linked to copper, expresses a desire for union, driving a soul toward the divine through the Path of Venus, the "wet path" of emotional and spiritual fusion. Mars, tied to iron, denotes a fiery will to overcome obstacles, resonating the Divine Plane's dynamic nature.

Planetary correspondences are not abstract but operative, requiring one to internalize and master their influences through rituals and inner work. For instance, the *Turba Philosophorum* advises an alchemist to "know the secret of the seven metals, for they are the keys to the kingdom," indicating each planet's essence must be integrated to unlock the cosmic order within.

The following ritual, rooted in Hermetic practice and Greek language, facilitates orientation to the divine *Nous*, fostering an actualized spiritual existence. It is designed for weekly practice, emphasizing contemplation and invocation to achieve a state of gnosis, supporting Evola's vision of spiritual transcendence. The ritual draws from the *Corpus Hermeticum* and *Greek Magical Papyri*, incorporating a Prayer of Thanksgiving to connect with the divine intelligence.

To prepare for the ritual, practitioners should select a quiet, dimly lit room facing north to signify illumination. The space should be free of distractions, ensuring a focused environment. Frankincense, a traditional incense noted in the *Asclepius* for its purifying qualities, should be burned to cleanse the space of negative energies. This ritual is best performed in early daylight upon waking, associating with the Hermetic link of morning to a presence of higher awareness.

Practitioners should wear a clean robe of white, symbolizing purity and divine radiance, made from natural fibers like cotton or linen to enhance energetic flow. An altar should be set up with a white candle to represent divine light, bowl of water for purification, and symbol of Hermes Trismegistus, such as a

Caduceus, to invoke his guidance. Practitioners should bathe to cleanse their body and aura, and perform the ritual fasted to enhance mental and spiritual clarity.

The ritual begins with a purification process to ensure the practitioner and space are free from impurities. Light the candle and frankincense, allowing a purifying essence to fill the room. Sprinkle a few drops of water from the bowl around the altar, creating a sacred boundary, and recite in Greek: "**Καθαρίζω τὸν χῶρον τοῦτον, ἵνα ἁγνὸς ᾖ πρὸς τὸ ἔργον τῆς σοφίας**" ("***Katharízō tòn chō̃ron toûton, hína hagnòs êi pròs tò érgon tês sophías***"), meaning "*I cleanse this space, that it may be pure for the work of wisdom.*" This establishes a consecrated setting, supporting the Hermetic tradition emphasizing spiritual cleanliness.

Take three deep breaths, inhaling via the nose and exhaling through the mouth, picturing a protective circle of light forming to shield against external influences. Next, invoke the heavenly *Nous* — source of all wisdom in Hermetic philosophy — to guide the ascent.

Standing before the altar, they raise their hands with palms upward, facing east, and recite: "**Νοῦς, θεῖον φῶς, φώτισόν με, ἵνα γνῶ τὴν ἀλήθειαν τοῦ ἑνός**" ("***Noûs, theîon phôs, phṓtisón me, hína gnō̃ tèn alḗtheian toû henósa***") meaning "*Nous, divine light, enlighten me, that I may know the truth of the One.*"

Speak while visualizing a golden light above, descending and entering through the crown of the head, filling the mind with clarity and godlike insight. This invocation, inspired by the *Corpus*

Hermeticum's emphasis on the *Nous* as Divine Mind, inaugurates a relationship with the transcendent, preparing a practitioner for the contemplative ascent.

The core of this ritual is a meditative journey through the planetary spheres, drawn from Hermetic texts like "The Key," wherein a soul ascends to achieve gnosis. The practitioner sits comfortably, either cross-legged or in a chair, closes their eyes, and starts breathing rhythmically: inhaling for four counts, holding for four, exhaling for four, and holding for four. This 4-4-4-4 pattern, repeated for four minutes, calms the mind and induces a light trance state conducive to spiritual work.

Visualize a golden ladder or staircase rising through the cosmos, each step corresponding to one of the seven planetary spheres: Saturn, Jupiter, Mars, Venus, Mercury, Moon, and Sun. At each sphere, release a specific attachment or quality binding them to the material world, allying with Evola's emphasis on transcending the lower self.

For Saturn, envision a dark void and release fear, reciting: "**Ἀπολύω τὸν φόβον**" ("***Apolúō tòn phóbōn***"), meaning "*I release fear,*" feeling liberated from distress.

For Jupiter, see a blue expanse and expel avarice, saying: "**Ἀπολύω τὴν πλεονεξίαν**" ("***Apolúō tèn pleonexían***"), meaning "*I release greed,*" embracing ease.

For Mars, visualize a red glow and discard antagonism, reciting: "**Ἀπολύω τὸν θυμόν**" ("***Apolúō tòn thymón***"), meaning "*I release anger,*" feeling hostility dissipate.

For Venus, envision a green radiance and let go of yearning, reciting: "**Ἀπολύω τὰς ἐπιθυμίας**" ("***Apolúō tàs epithumías***") meaning "*I release desires,*" feeling liberated from attachment.

For Mercury, visualize an auburn glow and shed mental chatter, saying: "**Ἀπολύω τὰς σκέψεις**" ("***Apolúō tàs sképseis***"), meaning "*I release thoughts.*" Identify the attention sharpening, cutting through ruminating intrusions and agitated thinking mired in futile abstraction.

For the Moon, visualize a silvery light and cast off emotional hastiness, reciting: "**Ἀπολύω τὴν συναισθηματικὴν ἀστάθειαν**" ("***Apolúō tèn sunaisthēmatikèn astátheian***"), meaning "*I release emotional instability.*" Imagine one's passions growing calm and balanced, like a still lake reflecting the luminosity.

For the Sun, see a golden brilliance and discharge trifling arrogance, speaking: "**Ἀπολύω τὴν ἐγωιστικὴν ὑπερηφάνειαν**" ("***Apolúō tèn egōistikèn huperēphánian***"), meaning "*I release egoic pride,*" and sensing the persona dissolve into sacred light.

Upon reaching the eighth sphere, beyond the planetary realms, the practitioner visualizes an unbounded, radiant light — the divine One. They relinquish the egoic self, merging with this light, and experience a profound sense of unity and gnosis. Recite: "**Ἐγὼ εἰμι τὸ φῶς, ἐγὼ εἰμι τὸ ἕν**" ("***Egò eimi tò phôs, egò eimi tò hén***"), meaning "*I am the light, I am the One.*"

They linger in this state for as long as feels natural, open to visions, insights, or a connection with sanctity. This moment aligns with Evola's vision of the Absolute Individual, where one abandons a lower egoic self to personify a godlike presence.

To conclude the ritual, offer gratitude using the Prayer of Thanksgiving from the *Asclepius* and *Greek Magical Papyri*. A cornerstone of Hermetic practice, this expresses gratitude for divine revelation, reinforcing a practitioner's connection to the transcendent. Standing before the altar, recite in Greek:

Εὐχαριστοῦμεν σοι, ὦ ἄρρητε ὄνομα, τὸ τιμώμενον ὡς θεός, τὸ αἰνούμενον ὡς πατήρ, ὅτι πᾶσιν καὶ πᾶσιν ἔδειξας πατρικὴν εὐσέβειαν, φιλίαν, ἀγάπην, καὶ γλυκυτάτην ἐνέργειαν, δωρούμενος ἡμῖν νοῦν, λόγον, γνῶσιν: νοῦν, ἵνα σε καταλάβωμεν· λόγον, ἵνα σε ἐπικαλεσώμεθα· γνῶσιν, ἵνα σε γνῶμεν.

"Efcharistoúmen soi, ó árrite ónoma, tó timómenon os theós, tó ainoúmenon os patír, óti pásin kaí pásin édeixas patrikín efséveian, filían, agápin, kaí glykytátin enérgeian, doroúmenos imín noún, lógon, gnósin: noún, ína se kataláνomen: lógon, ína se epikalesómetha: gnósin, ína se gnómen."

"We give thanks to you, o ineffable Name, honored as God and praised as Father, for to everyone and everything you have shown fatherly kindness, affection, love, and sweetest activity, granting to us mind, word, and knowledge: mind, that we may understand you; word, that we may call upon you; knowledge, that we may know you."

The practitioner then extinguishes the candle and incense, symbolizing the ritual's completion. They drink from the bowl of water, anchoring this experience in the physical body.

One must set a clear aim for spiritual growth, approaching the practice with reverence and sincerity. The ritual should be performed in a quiet, private space to minimize interruptions, and practitioners should avoid forcing visions or experiences, allowing insights to arise naturally.

One should incorporate this ritual into their training. Regular practice builds a cumulative effect, progressively instilling one with consecrated principles and fostering a realization of the Absolute Individual. This integration culminates in the Red Work, where the practitioner, having traversed the planetary spheres, returns to the Material Plane as a perfected being, embodying the ideal of *Rebis* — a unity of opposites.

The Cosmic Man's Indo-European legacy also manifests in the Greek Orphic tradition. There, a luminous "*protogenos*" named *Phanes* emerges from a cosmic egg to amalgamate light and form, symbolizing a divine potential within the human microcosm.

Similarly, the Avestan *Gayomart* (another primordial man) serves as a prototype for creation. His death seeds the world, with his essence offering a conduit to transcendence through initiatory knowledge.

These myths stress the Hermetic axiom that as a microcosm, a human being contains a blueprint for cosmic reintegration. Evola's *Theory of the Absolute Individual* frames this as a heroic act of self-overcoming wherein a practitioner, through alchemical and magical practices, reverses a celestial fall to reclaim their deific essence.

The four planes — Divine, Astral, Ethereal, and Material — thus serve as both a cosmological map and a practical itinerary. They outline an initiate's passage from the fragmented state of material existence to a unified state of the Absolute.

There, as the *Corpus Hermeticum* proclaims, "**ὁ νοῦς τοῦ θεοῦ γίνεται ἄνθρωπος**" ("*the mind of God becomes man*"). In this Hermetic cosmos, one becomes a living bridge between Heaven and Earth, typifying an eternal order through orderly transformation.

Practical Implements

Ritual tools and sacred space are potent symbols that bridge a practitioner's inner transformation with the outer cosmos. The Hermetic tradition emphasizes an operative power of ritual to awaken latent spiritual faculties, aligning an individual with the transcendent. The working tools — wand, dagger, cup, and pentacle — each embody elemental and metaphysical principles, serving as extensions of one's will and consciousness.

Similarly, the temple, altar, and circle form a sacred milieu demonstrating the microcosm-macrocosm correspondence and facilitating a process of self-realization. These accoutrements, infused with symbolic meaning enhanced by decorative motifs, are means for a practitioner to interface dynamically with the divine, embodying Evola's vision of magic as a disciplined path toward the Absolute Individual.

Connected with the element of fire, the wand exemplifies a practitioner's inspired potency. In *The Hermetic Tradition*, Evola describes this holy will as a driving force of transformation, akin to the alchemical fire that purifies and transfigures. Typically crafted from wood or metal and often adorned with symbols, the wand channels this burning energy to direct mystical forces during rituals.

It is used to invoke deities, project intention, or trace sigils in the air, aligning one's inner fire with potent archetypes. In the context of the *Greek Magical Papyri*, a wand might be inscribed with a solar symbol, such as the radiant circle found in spells to amplify its connection with divine authority and creative power. A practitioner wields the wand to assert their rule, embodying an active, masculine principle tied with spiritual heroism.

The dagger, linked to the element of air, symbolizes intellect and a power of discrimination. In Hermetic praxis, the mind must slash through illusions and mundane attachments to achieve lucidity, a process akin to the alchemical *Separatio*. Typically a double-edged blade, the dagger is used in rituals to eliminate undesirable influences, delineate sacred boundaries, or inscribe protective symbols.

Its airy nature aligns with the Astral Plane, where thoughts and archetypes take form, as described in *Introduction to Magic, Vol. I.* A practitioner might engrave a sigil on the dagger's handle to enhance its efficacy in warding off disruptive forces. By wielding the blade a magician sharpens their mental acuity, relating with Evola stressing intellectual rigor as a prerequisite for spiritual ascension.

The cup, corresponding to the element of water, embodies receptivity, intuition, and the subconscious. Evola connects the cup to the alchemical vessel, a symbol of the human heart and body that contains and transforms spiritual energies. In rituals, a cup holds consecrated liquids — water, wine, or other drinks — consumed as offerings or in communion with divine powers.

Its receptive quality renders it a tool for internal adjustment, as seen in the *Corpus Hermeticum*'s depiction as a receptacle for gnosis. One might inscribe the cup with a lunar symbol such as a crescent moon to enhance its connection to the Ethereal Plane's fluid luminosity. Through the cup, a magician engages emotional and intuitive dimensions, tempering will with receptivity in an alchemical union.

The pentacle, tied to the element of earth, represents the physical body and material reality, serving as a grounding force in ritual work. The material plane is an underpinning for spiritual expression where the alchemical *Coagulatio* stabilizes transformed energies. The pentacle, often a disc inscribed with a five-pointed star or other sigils, is placed on an altar to anchor energies and manifest intentions in the physical world.

In Introduction to Magic, Vol. II, the Ur Group emphasizes the use of symbols to focus consciousness, and a pentacle might bear a geometric figure such as an octagram to symbolize the microcosm's alignment with the greater cosmos. By meditating on archetypal symbols one incorporates their corporeal existence with superior planes, invoking the Hermetic principle of *Henosis*.

While not a primary tool, the robe serves as a ritual garment that separates a practitioner from the mundane world. Evola's emphasis on inner purity suggests a robe should be simple yet holy, perhaps adorned with symbols such as planetary sigils one is in harmony with. This augments the Great Work.

The creation of a sacred space — comprising temple, altar, and circle — is a mindful act of placing an external environment within one's magical universe. As a dedicated area, the sanctuary is a microcosm of an ordered universe — one free from profane distractions and imbued with sacrality. An external environment must reflect a practitioner's inner purity, a concept echoed in *Introduction to Magic, Vol. III*, where a ritual setting is described as a consecrated ambience.

The temple should be arranged to facilitate concentration, with minimal furnishings and complementary representations — such as planetary or alchemical sigils — painted or hung to evoke the proper energy. One prepares a space with cleansing methods using incense or perfumes as "condensers" for magical influences to create an atmosphere conducive to spiritual work.

The altar, positioned to face north, serves as the focal point of a temple, representing the direction of the midnight sun and source of divine light. An altar is the *axis mundi*, connecting one to divinity and grounding ritual activities. It is typically a simple table or platform draped with a cloth and adorned with the four ritual tools, candles, and offerings such as florae, talismans, or other sacred paraphernalia.

A northward orientation associates with the Indo-European emphasis on the polar axis. The altar's placement ensures that a practitioner faces the source of spiritual potency, reinforcing the microcosm-macrocosm correspondence central to Hermetic metaphysics.

The circle (whether physically drawn or visualized) defines a sacred enclosure within which ritual progresses. The circle is a protective barrier separating sacrosanct from secular, containing dynamisms invoked during magical operations. Inscribed with symbols such as the sigil of Mercury and Greek divine names, a perceivable circular emblem on the floor enhances conceptual visualization of the circle, making it a concrete focal point for one's intent.

Often drawn in chalk or Salt, this glyph mirrors the inner circle created in the "mind's eye," reinforcing a unity of internal and external realities. The circle's construction is a ritual act in itself, performed with a wand to trace its boundaries, invoking elemental or planetary forces to sanctify the space.

The integration of symbols from the *Greek Magical Papyri* into both tools and the ritual space enhances their esoteric potency. These antiquarian manuscripts provide a repository of sigils, deific appellations, and invocations that connect one to primordial magic currents. For illustration, a wand might be consecrated with the invocation "*IAO*," a powerful trinity of divine names, to amplify its authority.

Similarly, the circle might be inscribed with the "Barbarous Names" from the *Papyri*, chanted to evoke spiritual forces. These symbols, rooted in Greco-Egyptian tradition, resonate with Evola's emphasis on relinking with pre-Christian initiatic wisdom as seen in his rejection of devotional religion in favor of operative magic.

The use of these implements and spaces is not mechanical but deeply symbolic, requiring a practitioner to cultivate an inner state of purity and focus. Evola's magical idealism posits tools and setting are extensions of one's consciousness, serving to amplify their will and associate it with spiritual potencies.

When used with intention, wand, dagger, cup, and pentacle become conduits for a practitioner's spiritual faculties, enabling them to manipulate subtle energies and effect transformation. Likewise, the temple, altar, and circle create a structured setting that reflects one's internal sanctuary, facilitating an alchemical process of dissolving and coagulating the self into a higher state of being.

One's engagement with these utensils is guided by astrological timing and use of consecrated substances such as perfumes or herbs to enhance a ritual's efficacy. For instance, one performed under an influence of the Sun might use a wand inscribed with solar symbols, while a circle drawn during a lunar phase might incorporate water-related sigils to enhance intuitive work. Matching incenses may also be used, and so on.

Ultimately, these implements are tools for one to transcend the conditioned self. By wielding them inside a hallowed space, a magus engages in a dynamic interplay of microcosmic and macrocosmic forces. This exemplifies an idea of magic as a heroic path to spiritual autonomy, wherein one becomes a co-creator of reality while realizing their divine nature.

Solar Symbolism in Alchemy

Alchemy surpasses ordinary chemical procedures; it is a method of spiritual transformation, conduit to sovereignty, and means of becoming an Absolute Individual. Drawing upon his key work *The Hermetic Tradition*, Evola understands the Sun as a multifarious archetype corresponding to gold and its incorruptible essence, the procreative masculine principle, and a heavenly catalyst within all of humanity.

A solar motif permeates alchemical imagery — particularly in the forms of a lion and quadruple suns — serving as an operative vehicle along the initiatory path. These symbols demand active engagement, reflecting this Royal Art as grounded in the heroic spirituality of ancient Indo-Europeans.

The Sun's most immediate alchemical relationship is with gold, a perfected metal standing as an acknowledgement of nobility and incorruptibility. Evola describes this "Solar Body" as a purified, immortal essence distilled from the chaotic *Prima Materia* of self: a process that parallels an awakening of *Nous* — the divine intellect within. This is an active conquest where the alchemist, akin to a king, asserts dominion over both material and spiritual realms.

The masculine, generative power of the Sun finds resonance in Apollo, god of light and prophecy, whose clarity and foresight guide one throughout a labyrinth of transmutation. This solar dominion coincides with Evola's broader metaphysical framework in which the solar hero becomes an embodiment of deific command and counterforce to the materialist decline of modernity.

Among the vivid solar motifs, an image of a lion devouring the Sun occurs as a forceful symbol of primal energy harnessed for spiritual ends. In Evola's interpretation the lion represents a fiery, Sulfuric principle — an uncultivated masculine force that threatens to consume a practitioner's aspirations if unchecked. Yet, when mastered, this same energy becomes a catalyst for transformation.

The "green lion" in particular devours the Sun to extract its essence, symbolizing an abating of ego and purification of soul. This motif reiterates an Indo-European archetype of the solar hero who confronts and integrates tumultuous forces, a theme throughout Vedic, Hermetic, and other cosmologies. The act of devouring is not destruction but a sacrificial alteration where raw vigor is redirected toward creating a Solar Body.

The "black sun" or *sol niger* introduces a paradoxical depth to solar symbolism, marking the *Nigredo*: initial act of an alchemical *Magnum Opus*. This dark sun — linked to Saturn in Hermetic alchemy — signifies a descent into dissolution, a blackening of matter that unveils a hidden light within. Evola refers to it as the "sun behind the sun," a latent potential buried in the *Prima Materia*, akin to gold concealed within Saturn's leaden inertia.

This Saturnian sun resonates with a cyclical view of history, where the obscured truth of a primordial age awaits reactivation in one's initiatory work. The *Nigredo* occurs within a crucible. It is a conflict with a shadowy nature, setting the stage for illumination and reflecting a Hermetic principle of *solve et coagula* — dissolution followed by reintegration.

The four suns — black, white, yellow, and red — chart gradual stages of the *Magnum Opus*, each a milestone in a refinement of consciousness. The *sol niger* of *Nigredo* dissolves the ego, plunging one into darkness to unearth the divine spark. This is followed by *Albedo*, the white sun heralds purification and the awakening of inner light, a phase of ethereal clarity tied to the element of water.

Citrinitas, the yellow or golden sun, dawns as spiritual consciousness emerges. Its solar qualities of discernment and air-like intellect illuminate the path.

Finally, the *Rubedo*, the red sun, crowns the work with a realization of the Philosopher's Stone, a fiery union of opposites that births the Solar Body. Evola stresses a cyclical nature of these stages, where each dissolution fuels a higher restoration, aligning one with cosmic rhythms.

These solar symbols are not static icons but living forces within an alchemical vision. The lion's ferocity must be tamed through disciplined practice, its Sulfuric fire channeled into spiritual ascent. The four suns serve as a roadmap, each requiring proficiencies to navigate the elemental planes — earth, water, air, and fire — that constitute a practitioner's being.

This holistic amalgamation is a rejection of passive mysticism, supporting an active, heroic traversal of an initiatory path. An alchemist's work is a microcosmic battle wherein one strives toward sovereignty of self in alliance with divinity.

This analysis finds counterparts in other traditions, notably Taoism, where the "Golden Elixir" mirrors alchemical gold as the realization of the Immortal — a state of divine autonomy akin to the Solar Body. In *Taoism: The Magic, the Mysticism*, Evola draws a thread between an alchemical adept and Taoist sage, both transcending cycles of existence.

The *Corpus Hermeticum* emphasizes this with its call to discard physical attachment, a reiteration of the green lion's ego-dissolving feast. These cross-cultural echoes underscore the prevalence of solar symbolism as a beacon of transcendence, a motif existing in contrast to the Kali Yuga's spiritual darkness.

The alchemical Sun in its manifold expressions also carries a critique of modernity's egalitarian materialism. The sacred king adorned with the diadem of divine order stands in opposition to a chaotic leveling of contemporary culture. One's alignment with solar values reestablishes a hierarchical, spiritual authority and microcosmic reflection of macrocosmic harmony.

This transformative potential is practical. An alchemist must internalize these symbols through rigorous discipline. The lion and suns become tools of self-realization, unlocking mysteries of both self and the universe.

The solar motif extends further into the esoteric practices of the alchemical tradition, particularly in the context of ritual and visualization. Evola emphasizes an importance of one's internal alignment with the Sun's radiant energy, often achieved through meditative techniques that evoke solar imagery. In *Introduction to Magic, Vol. II*, he describes rituals where an adept visualizes a solar disc within the heart, a practice that concentrates spiritual fire to burn away impurities.

This inner sun becomes the focal point of transformation: a radiant center that aligns a practitioner's awareness with the cosmic axis. Such practices draw from the *Greek Magical Papyri*, where solar invocations — such as those addressing Helios with divine names like "*IAO*" — amplify one's connection to the solar principle, reinforcing their sacred authority.

Moreover, the Sun's role as a propagative force connects to Evola's conception of the "heroic" path wherein an alchemist assumes the mantle of a spiritual warrior. The lion devouring the Sun can be seen as a metaphor for an adept's confrontation with their instinctual drives: a battle to sublimate base desires into divine will.

This struggle is not merely psychological but metaphysical, requiring a practitioner to harness the solar fire to transcend the limitations of the material self. Evola's importance on this active engagement distinguishes his methodology from those more docile mystic traditions, aligning with his broader notion of a spiritual aristocracy.

The black sun also carries cosmological implications in Evola's framework, particularly its association with Saturn and the cyclical nature of time. In *The Hermetic Tradition*, he alludes to ancient myths where Saturn, as a primeval solar deity, ruled a Golden Age before its light was obfuscated by decline. The alchemist's task is to rediscover this hidden sun, reactivating its latent power through *Nigredo's* transformative darkness.

This process reflects Evola's view of history as a descent from a primordial, solar order into the entropy of our modern era, a perspective shared by René Guénon in *The Great Triad*. The black sun thus becomes a symbol of hope. It serves as a reminder that even in the depths of spiritual night the solar essence endures, awaiting rediscovery by a resolute adept.

The four suns further elaborate this transformative journey, each corresponding to a planetary influence the alchemist must integrate. The yellow sun of *Citrinitas* ties to the planet Jupiter, signifying expansive insight and illumination of consciousness. This stage requires a practitioner to cultivate intellectual clarity, a quality that resonates with the airy element and an Apollonian ideal of rational insight.

Linked to Mars, the red sun of *Rubedo* embodies a fiery apex of the work in which one's will is forged into an inflexible power of dominion.

These planetary correspondences help highlight an alchemical process as a cosmic ascent. Through it a practitioner navigates the celestial hierarchy to achieve union with the divine.

Solar symbolism transcends its material referents, becoming an ontological map for an alchemical pilgrimage. The Sun's association with gold is not about wealth, but an incorruptible essence. The lion's devouring act is a rite of purification and the four suns are a ladder to the Absolute.

Each symbol interlocks within a context of transformation and sovereignty, guiding a practitioner toward a state where one's divine spark blazes fully realized. Through this royal art, Evola envisions an alchemist as a warrior of the spirit wielding solar power to forge an immortal destiny.

Preliminary Exercises and Ritual Praxis

A series of preliminary exercises and regular rituals form a systematic path to spiritual transformation and an ultimate goal of *Henosis* — union with the deific. These practices are designed to refine one's awareness, unite with cosmic order, and realize the Absolute Individual.

The practice of "Opus Magicum: Concentration and Silence," detailed by Luce in *Introduction to Magic, Volume I*, serves as a foundational exercise for cultivating mental clarity and inner stillness. This training is vital for detaching from the incessant chatter of one's mundane mind and facing the ego's dominance, aligning with the alchemical stage of *Nigredo* — dissolution of impurities and engagement with the shadow self.

In Hermetic theology, purification of mind is a prerequisite for divine perception, as stated in the Corpus Hermeticum: "**Νοῦς ὁ καθαρὸς οὐκ ἔστιν ὑπὸ τῶν παθῶν κατακρατούμενος**" ("The pure mind is not dominated by passions"). This exercise prepares a practitioner for deeper spiritual work by fostering a state of inner calm and focus, essential for transcending the material self — one's lesser incantatory state.

To perform Concentration and Silence, a practitioner should select a quiet, dimly lit space free from distractions. This ideally is a dedicated room or area reserved for spiritual practice (one's temple).

Sit in a comfortable upright position, such as cross-legged on a zabuton (cushion) or in a chair with feet on the floor, maintaining alertness. Soften the gaze, focusing on a sole point of attention. This could be a physical object such as a candle, Hermetic emblem (e.g., Caduceus), or related celestial image like a star octagram. The goal is to anchor the intellect to this point, gently redirecting it without judgment or attachment when thoughts arise.

Begin with 8 minutes daily, progressively extending to 12 minutes as skill increases. The practice should be conducted in total outward silence, with inner calm achieved by observing thoughts as fleeting spectacles, allowing them to dissolve. Over time, this cultivates a state of mental clarity in which one can access deeper layers of awareness, confronting and integrating the shadow qualities of identity. This associates with *Nigredo's* transformative dissolution, clearing persona to reveal a distilled essence beneath.

The "Instructions for the 'Awareness of Breath'" by Abraxas, also from *Volume I*, builds on the mental clarity established in Concentration and Silence by enhancing awareness of a subtle character — an energetic conduit between physical and spiritual realms. This practice grounds one in the present, promoting a heightened understanding of the life-force (*pneuma* or *prana*) animating existence.

It relates to the alchemical stage of *Albedo*, denoting distillation and a spiritual awakening wherein one begins to connect with their highest nature. The *Greek Magical Papyri* emphasize the breath's role in ritual, where controlled breathing activates a practitioner's spiritual potency: "**Πνεῦμα τὸ ζῶν, τὸ συνέχον τὰ πάντα**" ("The living breath, holding all things together").

To practice Awareness of Breath, find a quiet space and assume a comfortable seated or lying position, ensuring the spine is straight to facilitate energy flow. Close the eyes and bring attention to the natural rhythm of the breath, observing the sensation of air entering and exiting the nostrils or the rise and decrease of the chest. Do not attempt to control or alter the breath; instead, maintain a passive awareness, noting its texture, temperature, and regularity. If the mind wanders, gently return focus to the breath without frustration.

Practice for 8-12 minutes daily, ideally in the afternoon to balance the day's energies. As awareness deepens, one may sense vibrations or warmth, indicating activation of the subtle body. This repetition purifies a practitioner's energetic field, invoking *Albedo's* radiance and preparing for advanced esoteric work by grounding spiritual awareness in the physical form.

Visualization practices involve mentally constructing and engaging with Hermetic symbols or scenes — such as those from the *Emerald Tablet* — to internalize principles of cosmic balance and spiritual ascent. This exercise relates to the alchemical stage of *Citrinitas*, where spiritual wisdom is integrated, leading to clarity and insight.

To engage in Hermetic Visualization, set aside 8-12 minutes in the evening, in a quiet space with minimal lighting to enhance focus. Sit comfortably and close the eyes, beginning with a few minutes of deep breathing to center the mind. Select a Hermetic symbol, such as the Caduceus. Visualize the representation vividly, imagining its colors, shapes, and energetic presence.

For illustration, envision the Caduceus as a golden staff with interweaving serpents, radiating luminance. Immerse yourself in its meaning, contemplating its connection to cosmic harmony and your own spiritual ascent. Alternatively, visualize a scene from the *Emerald Tablet*, such as the union of heaven and earth, feeling the interplay of macrocosm and microcosm within. If the mind wanders, gently return to the image.

The practice of "Opus Magicum: The 'Words of Power' and the Characters of Beings" by Luce, found in *Volume I*, harnesses vocalized intent to activate spiritual forces. This involves reciting mantras, sacred words, or invocations that resonate with specific energies or entities, enhancing ritual efficacy and deepening metaphysical connections. It invokes the alchemical stage of *Rubedo*, where fusion with the divine is realized, and a practitioner embodies the Absolute Individual. The *Corpus Hermeticum* highlights a creative power of speech: "**Λόγος ὁ δημιουργὸς τῶν ὄντων**" ("*The Word, creator of all things*").

Engage the Words of Power training once weekly, organizing a ritual space with candles, incense (e.g., frankincense), and a small altar displaying a Hermetic symbol. Select a consecrated word or phrase like "*As above, so below*" from the *Emerald Tablet* or a divine name such as "ΙΑΩ" ("*IAO*") from the *Greek Magical Papyri*. Sit or stand before the altar, center yourself with a few deep breaths, and begin intoning a chosen word or phrase with clear intention, focusing on its vibrational quality.

Chant rhythmically for 4-8 minutes, allowing the sound to resonate within and connect with spiritual forces. Visualize the word's energy radiating outward, aligning your being with the divine. This practice amplifies spiritual power, facilitating communion with higher realms.

A structured schedule integrates each of these practices into daily and weekly routines following this timetable:

Daily Practices

Morning (Concentration and Silence): In a discreet space, focus on a single point (e.g., candle flame) to cultivate mental clarity, aligning with *Nigredo's* purification.

Afternoon (Awareness of Breath): Observe the breathing's rhythm to ground it in the present, fostering *Albedo's* spiritual awakening.

Evening (Hermetic Visualization): Visualize a symbol (e.g., Caduceus) to summon celestial energies, embodying *Citrinitas'* wisdom.

Weekly Practice

Words of Power: In a ritual setting, repeat a sacred phrase (e.g., "As above, so below") to activate spiritual forces, advancing toward *Rubedo.*

This regimen guarantees steady progress, with each practice building on the previous to cultivate inner faculties necessary for *Henosis*. Practitioners should maintain a dedicated journal to track experiences and insights, modifying the schedule as required while ensuring consistency.

The "Instructions for Ceremonial Magic" by Luce, likewise in *Volume I*, represent a culmination of the preliminary exercises, involving elaborate rituals to invoke spiritual entities and harness spiritual powers for transformation. This practice requires mental clarity, subtle body awareness, and spiritual alignment developed through preceding exercises, facilitating direct interaction with metaphysical realms.

It parallels the final stage of *Rubedo*, in which a practitioner realizes the Philosopher's Stone — a symbolic depiction of the Absolute Individual. *The Greek Magical Papyri* feature such rituals, involving precise incantations and tools to commune with heavenly authorities: "**Επικαλοῦμαι σε, τὸν μέγαν θεόν**" ("***Epikaloumài se, tòn Mégan Theón***") meaning, "*I invoke you, the Great God.*"

To perform a grand ritual, prepare a sacred space with an altar adorned with Hermetic symbols, candles, incense, and ritual tools.

Begin with purification by bathing. Center yourself with Concentration and Silence, followed by Awareness of Breath, to fortify your dynamism. Perform visualizations to connect with the Hermetic current, then recite Words of Power drawing from texts like the *Greek Magical Papyri*. Repeat "**ΊΑΩ Σαβαώθ**" ("***IÁŌ Sabaṓth***") while picturing a white light enveloping the space.

Follow with a planned invocation, such as a prayer to Hermes Trismegistus, and end with a reflection on the ritual's effects. This preparation facilitates transformation via an alchemical process.

Evola's approach, as articulated in *The Hermetic Tradition*, views alchemy as a universal science of transformation, distinct from mere chemistry or psychological individuation. The UR Group's practices in *Introduction to Magic* underscored self-transmutation through discipline and willpower. *The Corpus Hermeticum* and *Greek Magical Papyri* provide foundational writings, with precepts like "**Γνῶθι σεαυτόν**" ("*Know thyself*") underscoring an introspective journey.

These exercises demand intermediate esoteric proficiency, rendering them suitable for dedicated practitioners. Beginners should inaugurate with Concentration and Silence, gradually incorporating other practices as proficiency grows. Access to principal texts, such as *Introduction to Magic* and the *Corpus Hermeticum*, is essential for precise instructions.

Practitioners should construct a devoted space free of diversion. They likewise ought to approach each exercise with reverence and commitment.

Challenges may include maintaining focus, overcoming mental resistance, or navigating an intensity (at times overwhelming) of ceremonial operations. Regular contemplation and guidance from experienced practitioners can mitigate these obstacles, ensuring a devotion to one's spiritual course.

These principal exercises and sacraments offer a comprehensive framework for spiritual progress. Through disciplined practice one purifies the soul, awakens to greater truths, and integrates godlike sentience to achieve *Henosis*.

The Vertical Axis

Spiritual actualization entails galvanizing subtle physiology, thereby transforming one's self through disciplined practice into an Absolute Individual. The Ritual of the Vertical Axis offers a practical method to activate and harmonize these centers of power — akin to chakras — using planetary correspondences.

This ritual employs the seven classical planets (Sun, Moon, Mercury, Venus, Mars, Jupiter, and Saturn) mapped to specific centers along the body's vertical axis, each tied to an alchemical metal: gold, silver, Mercury, copper, iron, tin, and lead. The practice refines one's subtle makeup, enflaming the "body of fire," and progressing it toward the "resurrected body," personifying a Hermetic principle of micro and macrocosmic correspondence as articulated in the *Emerald Tablet.*

The spirit's physiology, as outlined in *Introduction to Magic, Vol. I,* consists of layered energetic structures. It comprises the etheric double, which sustains physical vitality; an astral body, governing attitudes and imagination; the mental body, seat of intellect; and a causal body, one's enduring spiritual essence. These layers converge at seven centers along the vertical axis, each resonating with a planetary influence and its alchemical metal.

The crown, at the head's apex, corresponds to the Sun and gold, radiating divine vitality. The third eye, between the brows, aligns with the Moon and silver, enhancing intuitive perception. The throat, tied to Mercury and quicksilver, facilitates smooth expression. The heart, linked to Venus and copper, harmonizes emotional and spiritual integration. The solar plexus, associated with Mars and iron, fuels assertive will. The sacral center, below the navel, reverberates with Jupiter and tin, sparking productive expansion. The root, at the spine's base, anchors with Saturn and lead, ensuring constancy. As Arthur Versluis emphasizes in *The Philosophy of Magic,* this configuration reflects the Hermetic axiom "as above, so below," positioning one as cosmic mirror.

To perform the Ritual of the Vertical Axis, select a peaceful space free of distractions where the spine can remain straight — standing or seated on a stable surface. A single candle and Hermetic symbol such as the Caduceus may enhance focus, but inner intent is paramount. Begin with rhythmic breathing (inhale for four counts, hold for four, exhale for four, and hold for four, repeating for four minutes) calming the mind and attuning to subtle energies. Visualize a sphere of pure white light hovering one foot above the head, embodying the *Prima Materia* — an unmanifest source of all forces. This sphere operates as origin point for planetary energies that will flow through the centers, activating one's subtle physiology.

Start at the crown, where a golden sphere forms, infused with the Sun's radiant vitality. Inhale, drawing light from the *Prima Materia*; exhale, intoning "*Sol*" in a resonant tone, feeling the sphere blaze with golden light. Shift to the third eye, where a silver sphere materializes, pulsating with the Moon's reflective intuition. Inhale, channeling energy from the crown; exhale, reciting "*Luna*" and sharpening clarity. At the throat, an orange sphere forms — Mercury's flowing intellect. Inhale, energy drifts downward; exhale, "*Mercurius*" activates expressive flow.

The heart awakens as a copper sphere, Venus' harmonious essence. Inhale, pulling energy through; exhale, "*Venus*" radiates warmth and integration. The solar plexus enflames with a red sphere, Mars' iron resolution. Inhale, energy descends; exhale, "*Mars*" strengthens will. The sacral center glows blue, Jupiter's expansive tin. Inhale, continuing the current; exhale, "*Jupiter*" sparks creativity. At the root, a black sphere solidifies, Saturn's leaden anchor. Inhale grounding energy, exhaling "*Saturnus*."

With all centers activated, visualize a continuous current of light flowing from crown to root, then looping skyward in an uninterrupted circuit. Maintain this for several minutes, first in silent focus and then intoning the planetary sequence: *Sol, Luna, Mercurius, Venus, Mars, Jupiter, Saturnus*. The axis becomes a blazing pillar with one's subtle body fully stimulated, igniting the "body of fire."

This intense state, a synthesis of etheric and astral energies increased by solar potency, functions as a medium for spiritual transformation. Conclude at the heart, where the copper sphere fortifies, integrating all planetary influences. Affirm, "*I am the vertical axis, uniting earth and cosmos, refined in the alchemical fire of the self.*" Repose in stillness for a moment, absorbing the transformation before returning to ordinary awareness.

This ritual enacts the alchemical *Magnum Opus* wherein a practitioner becomes a receptacle for alteration, as delineated by Mircea Eliade in *Forge and the Crucible.* The white light's image initiates *Calcinatio*, purifying intent; the downward energy flow parallels *Solutio*, dissolving blockages; the intonations proclaim *Coagulatio*, binding energies; and the heart's integration reflects *Sublimatio*, elevating the self to a higher state. The "resurrected body," referenced in *Introduction to Magic, Vol. III*, emerges as the subtle physiology refined to its fullest potential: a state of spiritual invincibility embodying the Philosopher's Stone.

Regular practice strengthens one's subtle physiology, in turn enhancing clarity and resilience. By concentrating on planetary energies, the ritual aligns with the *Greek Magical Papyri's* use of celestial forces for transformation, making the practitioner a living *axis mundi*, harmonizing microcosm and macrocosm. To strengthen the exercise, cultivate *hyperstasis* (a heightened awareness) with preparatory features like fasting and ritualized washing.

The *Soma Psychikon* is the psychic body: a subtle vehicle of conscious spiritual awareness. The ritual's planetary activations strengthen this layer, associating it with cosmic hierarchy and purifying the soul as a dynamic entity. The "solar principle" unifies the axis as an individuating fire, making the practitioner a *Homo Solis*. The *Magnum Opus* advances within, culminating in a "resurrected body."

Invoking the Elements

The elements — Earth, Water, Air, and Fire — are principles connecting an external cosmos to the inner self. These forces represent both states of consciousness and transformation, essential for achieving an actualized spiritual existence. The elemental invocation is an induction achieved through a detailed pathworking: a pointed visualization immersing a practitioner in symbolic landscapes to internalize each element's sacred essence. Drawing from a vision of these elements as catalyzing principles, this process fosters a profound connection to their transcendent qualities.

Pathworking Steps

Preparation: Begin standing in a quiet area facing north. Enter a relaxed state with deep, rhythmic breathing. Visualize yourself in a neutral sacred space, such as a stone temple or a void of light, symbolizing the unmanifest potential within.

Earth (West): Turn to the West and envision a dense forest surrounding a towering mountain. Feel the solid earth beneath your feet, its weight anchoring you. Imagine roots extending from your body into the ground, drawing up stability and potency. Reflect on Earth as the alchemical *Nigredo* — the dark, foundational matter from which transformation begins.

Take time embodying this groundedness. Afterward, recite: **"Καλέω σε, στοιχεῖον τῆς Γῆς, ἄρχοντα τῆς Δύσεως. Δός μοι τὴν σταθερότητα καὶ τὴν γονιμότητα"** ("***Kaléō se, stoicheîon tês Gês, árchonta tês Dúseōs. Dós moi tèn statherótēta kaì tèn gonimótēta***"), meaning "*I call upon you, element of Earth, ruler of the West. Grant me firmness and fecundity.*"

Water (South): Face South and picture a vast sea with its waves lapping effortlessly. Step into the water, feeling its transformative power envelop you, cleansing away inferiority. Merge with its currents, embracing poise and depth — this is akin to the alchemical *Albedo*, the purification stage.

Linger here a moment, internalizing its cleansing essence. Then intone: **"Καλέω σε, στοιχεῖον τοῦ Ὕδατος, ἄρχοντα τῆς Νότου. Δός μοι τὴν ρευστότητα καὶ τὴν καθαρότητα"** ("***Kaléō se, stoicheîon toû Hýdatos, árchonta tês Nótou. Dós moi tèn rheustótēta kaì tèn katharótēta***"), meaning "*I call upon you, element of Water, ruler of the South. Grant me fluidity and purity.*"

Air (East): Turn East and visualize an expansive sky, the wind swirling around you. Inhale deeply, sensing clarity and freedom as you rise above worldly concerns. Imagine soaring like a bird, typifying the alchemical *Citrinitas* — sacred ascent.

Absorb this lightness for a time. Subsequently, proclaim: **"Καλέω σε, στοιχεῖον τοῦ Ἀέρος, ἄρχοντα τῆς Ἀνατολῆς. Δός μοι τὴν σαφήνεια καὶ τὴν ἐλευθερία"** ("***Kaléō se, stoicheîon toû Aéros, árchonta tês Anatolês. Dós moi tèn saphéneian kaì tèn eleutherían***"), meaning "*I call upon you, element of Air, ruler of the East. Grant me clarity and freedom.*"

Fire (North): Face North and see a blazing sun with its searing heat radiating toward you. Step closer, becoming a flame yourself and burning away impurities with intensity. This is the alchemical *Rubedo*, a red culmination of the Great Work.

Feel the power for several minutes, radiating will and vitality. Afterward recite: **"Καλέω σε, στοιχεῖον τοῦ Πυρός, ἄρχοντα τῆς Βορρᾶ. Δός μοι τὴν ἐνέργεια καὶ τὴν μεταμόρφωσιν"** ***("Kaléo se, stoicheíon toú Pyrós, árchonta tís Vorrá. Dós moi tín enérgeia kaí tín metamórfosin")***, meaning *"I call upon you, element of Fire, ruler of the North. Emblazon the spirit within me."*

Integration: Visualize the four elements converging within you — Earth's roots, Water's tide, Air's draught, and Fire's heat — harmonizing into a balanced whole. Affirm your alignment with the cosmos, reposing in this unison for a decisive, prolonged moment. Conclude with: **"Ὡς ἄνω, οὕτως κάτω"** ***("Os áno, oútos káto")***, meaning *"As above, so below."*

This Hermetic axiom impresses the ritual, affirming an accord of microcosm and macrocosm.

When practiced with intent, this pathworking affiliates one's inner bearing with these elemental forces, fostering an actualized spiritual existence as Evola envisioned — a state where the self personifies a metaphysical hierarchy.

The Greek invocations emulate the style of the *Greek Magical Papyri*, where practitioners called upon powers with phrases like "**Καλέω σε**" ("*I call upon you*") to establish connection. While the PGM often invokes deities, this ritual adapts the form to address the elements directly, aligning with Evola's focus on their operative significance.

Performed daily, this ritual takes 10-15 minutes and reinforces a practitioner's bond with the elements. It cultivates stability (Earth), transformation (Water), clarity (Air), and will (Fire), aligning with Evola's ideal of spiritual actualization. Over time, this repetition refines a practitioner's inner state, making them a living conduit for cosmic forces. Its simplicity, requiring no tools beyond intent and voice, ensures accessibility, though optional symbols (e.g., a stone for Earth, a candle for Fire) may enhance focus if desired.

Foundation for Advanced Workings

As a preliminary step, this ritual consecrates a space and purifies the practitioner's consciousness, creating a balanced elemental foundation for advanced Hermetic practices. For example:

Planetary Invocations: After invoking the elements, call upon a planetary force (e.g., Mars for will), leveraging an established foundation.

Theurgic Rituals: Use the ritual to attune to divine energies, as elements are seen in Hermeticism as emanations of the divine mind (*Corpus Hermeticum*).

Alchemical Operations: Treat the ritual as a symbolic preparation of the *Prima Materia*, readying oneself for inner transmutation.

By grounding a practitioner in the elements, it amplifies the efficacy of subsequent workings, embodying magic as a path to transcendence. Through daily engagement, it prepares one for the Great Work. It offers a disciplined path to transmutation rooted in authentic traditions and adaptable to advanced rituals. As a cornerstone of Evolian Hermetic practice it establishes a dynamic alignment with the primal forces of Earth, Water, Air, and Fire, anchoring one in cosmic order.

The *Pneuma*, a central concept in the *Corpus Hermeticum*, is the divine breath or spiritual essence permeating all existence, linking the material elements to a universal *Nous* (Divine Mind). In a ritualized elemental invocation, rhythmic breathing and sacred recitations channel this force, infusing a practitioner's subtle body with vital energy.

The *Greek Magical Papyri* often emphasize breath as a conduit for divine power, suggesting a ritual's breathing pattern as an active invocation of the *Pneuma*. By consciously directing breath during the pathworking, one links their vitality with elemental forces, creating a resonant circuit that reproduces a universal synchrony. This strengthens the subtle body, enabling it to act as a vessel for higher awareness.

The alchemical *Quinta Essentia* (fifth essence) represents a unifying principle beyond the four elements, often associated with ether or the divine spark within. As Mircea Eliade notes in *The Forge and the Crucible*, the quintessence is the goal of an alchemical opus, synthesizing elemental qualities into a transcendent whole.

During the ritual's integration phase in which one visualizes a convergence of Earth, Water, Air, and Fire, the *Quinta Essentia* is symbolically realized. This act, sealed with a recitation of "**Ὠς ἄνω, οὕτως κάτω**" ("*As above, so below*"), invokes the Hermetic principle of unity, positioning a practitioner as the cosmic axis. Evola's *The Hermetic Tradition* emphasizes this synthesis as key to spiritual transformation, where the elements are not merely balanced but transcended, forming a higher state of being akin to the "body of fire" referenced in *Introduction to Magic, Vol. I.* Daily ritual practice cultivates this inner alchemy, refining one's substance into the *Quinta Essentia.*

Inner polarity, a concept implied in Evola's discussions of spiritual differentiation in *Introduction to Magic, Vol. II*, refers to a dynamic tension between active and receptive forces within the self. The ritual engages this polarity by balancing the elements' qualities: Earth's corporeality (receptive) with Air's ephemerality (active), and Water's fluidity (receptive) with Fire's resolve (active). This interplay mirrors the alchemical marriage of opposites, a process Evola describes as essential for achieving spiritual sovereignty.

By invoking each element in its cardinal direction — Earth (West), Water (South), Air (East), Fire (North) — the practitioner internalizes these polarities, creating a dynamic equilibrium that promotes self-mastery. The *Greek Magical Papyri* often structure rituals around directional invocations to harness such polarities, demonstrating that a ritual's schema amplifies its transmutative power.

To enhance a ritual's efficacy, practitioners may incorporate a preparatory meditative focus on the *Pneuma* before beginning, visualizing breath as a luminous thread connecting self to the cosmos. Additionally, maintaining a ritual log to note things like shifts in perception or energy during a pathworking can deepen awareness of the *Quinta Essentia*'s emergence.

Performed daily, these practices reinforce a ritual's role as a foundation for advanced workings, like planetary invocations or theurgic rites, by establishing a balanced elemental framework. Through the *Pneuma*, *Quinta Essentia*, and one's inner polarity, this elemental invocation becomes a living process of spiritual actualization, giving one a path toward realizing Evola's vision of the Absolute Individual.

Planetary Magic

Planetary magic is part of a disciplined path toward spiritual actualization, transforming the practitioner through orientation with celestial bodies. Ritual facilitates inner alignment with the planets: Saturn (Lead), Jupiter (Tin), Mars (Iron), Venus (Copper), Mercury (Quicksilver), Moon (Silver), Sun (Gold), and Neptune (Platinum). Designed for weekly practice, it serves as a basis for advanced workings, embodying the microcosmic-macrocosmic coherence central to Hermeticism.

Subtle physiology comprises layered energetic structures: an etheric double sustaining physical vitality; the astral body governing emotions and imagination; a mental body, seat of intellect; and the causal body, an enduring spiritual essence. These layers intersect at seven centers along the body's vertical axis, each resonating with a planetary influence and its alchemical metal, with an additional force influencing the outer aura via Neptune.

Saturn (Lead) at the root grounds stability; Jupiter (Tin) at the sacral center sparks expansion; Mars (Iron) at the solar plexus fuels resolve; Venus (Copper) at the heart fosters coherence; Mercury (Quicksilver) at the throat sharpens expression; the Moon (Silver) at the third eye enhances intuition; the Sun (Gold) at the crown radiates divine will; and Neptune (Platinum), enveloping the outer aura, evokes transcendent inspiration. This configuration, inspired by the *Emerald Tablet's* axiom "as above, so below," situates the practitioner as a reflection of the cosmos.

The proceeding ritual invokes these forces before an altar using recitations inspired by the *Greek Magical Papyri.* This planetary induction synchronizes one with the celestial forces, cultivating their spiritual qualities.

Begin in a quiet, dimly lit space, facing north and standing with a straight spine. Arrange an altar with eight talismans: a black stone (Saturn), blue jewel (Jupiter), red edge (Mars), green rod (Venus), orange plume (Mercury), silver crescent (Moon), golden disc (Sun) and indigo mineral (Neptune). Suitable augmentations like incense (e.g., frankincense for the Sun and myrrh for Saturn) or symbols (e.g., octagram as two interlinking squares, symbolizing the eight planets) are encouraged.

Enter a meditative state with rhythmic breathing: inhale for four counts, hold for four, exhale for four, hold for four, and repeat. Standing before the altar, center yourself with four deep breaths. Invoke each planet by lighting its candle and holding its associated object, reciting:

Saturn: "**Καλέω σε, Κρόνε, χρόνου ἄρχοντα, δὸς μοι τὴν ὑπομονήν**" ("***Kaléō se, Krónē, chrónou árchonta, dòs moi tèn hupomonḗn***"), meaning, "*I call upon you, Kronos, lord of time, grant me endurance.*" Closing the eyes, focus on a black sphere at the perineum and envision oneself in a dark cave drawing tenacity. Eyes open, ground in Saturn's stability at the root.

This is a grave summons to *Kronos*, austere Lord of Time, devourer of ages and father of order through limitation. Not the whining patience of the weak, but an iron endurance of one who stands immovable amid corrosion of becoming — the capacity to wait without yielding, to bear the slow grinding of cosmic necessity without complaint or haste. *Kronos* teaches that true power is measured in epochs, not moments; his gift is the virile fortitude that scorns the ephemeral.

Jupiter: "**Καλέω σε, Ζεῦ, βασιλεῦ τῶν θεῶν, δὸς μοι τὴν μεγαλοπρέπειαν**" ("***Kaléō se, Zeû, basileû tôn theôn, dòs moi tèn megaloprepeian***"), meaning, "*I call upon thee, Zeus, king of the gods, grant me greatness.*" Imagine a blue sphere at the navel on a mountain summit incorporating expansive energy. Internalize Jupiter's prominence at the sacral center.

This is no appeal for inflated ego or profane ambition, which is the very antithesis of what *Zeus* embodies. It is the quality of a differentiated man who lives on a scale commensurate with the eternal: grandeur of bearing, magnificence of spirit, the capacity to manifest a superior principle without conciliation or decline. It is the regal quality *Zeus* himself incarnates as the thunderer who orders the cosmos — a sovereign who tolerates no equivalence with the lower orders.

To invoke *Zeus* for this gift is to demand alignment with the very summit of the Olympian hierarchy: not to become "great" in the eyes of men, but participate in the impersonal Greatness descending from the Principle and radiating through the rightly ordered king, hero, and initiate who has transcended a servile horizon of quantity and utility.

Mars: "**Καλέω σε, Ἄρη, πολέμου κύριε, δὸς μοι τὴν δύναμιν**" ("***Kaléō se, Árē, polémou kúrie, dòs moi tèn dúnamin***"), meaning, "*I call upon you, Ares, lord of war, grant me strength.*" Visualize a red sphere at your solar plexus, the self in a forge summoning iron will. Channel Mars' resolve at the solar plexus.

Ares is a virile, furious impulse of martial force — not chaos, but a disciplined fury that breaks resistance and imposes form through conflict. His gift is raw, impersonal power: the capacity to act decisively, to strike without hesitation, to embody the warrior principle that defends sacred order against dissolution.

Venus: "**Καλέω σε, Φωσφόρε, ἑωσφόρε φωτός, δὸς μοι τὴν ἀκεραιότητα.**" ("***Kaléō se, Phōsphóre, heōsphóre phōtós, dòs moi tèn akeraíotēta***"), meaning, "*I call upon thee, Phosphoros, light-bearer of the dawn, grant me integrity.*" See a green sphere at your heart, then oneself within a lush garden embracing virtue. Exemplify Venus' luminescence at the core.

Phōsphoros is the Morning Star — herald of dawn and principle of illumination that precedes the full solar ascent. In the primeval tradition, *Phōsphoros* (also named *Eosphoros*) is the "Luciferian" aspect in its unpolluted, pre-descent sense. Bearer of primordial light, a star which pierces the darkness of night without being the sun itself, and symbol of an initiatic intellect that rises before the vulgar day.

The requested quality is **ἀκεραιότητα** (***akeraíotēta***): integrity in an essential and aristocratic sense — not ethical "honesty" or bourgeois uprightness, but an unbroken wholeness of being, the incorruptible coherence of Self that remains singular and undivided amid every trial, temptation, or dispersion. It is the adamantine fidelity to one's own principle; a refusal of all compromise with the subordinate orders and an internal rectitude that renders a man impermeable to subversion from without or decay from within.

Integrity here is effective metaphysical fidelity: a capacity to remain centered in light even when surrounded by the shadows of multiplicity and becoming. To invoke the Morning Star for this gift is to demand an interior dawn that dissipates illusion without sentimentality — the sharp, unyielding clarity that knows itself as a ray of the eternal and refuses to bend.

Mercury: "**Καλέω σε, Ἑρμῆ, νοῦν ταχύν, δὸς μοι τὴν εὐελιξίαν**" ("***Kaléō se, Hermê, noûn tachún, dòs moi tèn euelixían***"), meaning, "*I call upon thee, Hermes, swift of mind, grant me quick-wittedness.*" Focus on an orange sphere at your throat, oneself on a windswept plain imbibing eloquence. Absorb Mercury's perceptual agility at the throat.

Hermes is psychopomp, boundary-crosser, and master of swift intelligence and subtle mediation. His gift is a mental dexterity that penetrates veils, adapts without losing center, and traverses realms with Olympian ease. Not cunning for its own sake, but a luminous agility of intellect that serves higher ends.

Moon: "**Καλέω σε, Σελήνη, νυκτὸς ἄρχουσα, δὸς μοι τὴν διαισθητικότητα**" ("***Kaléō se, Selḗnē, nuktòs árchousa, dòs***

moi tèn diaisthētikótēta") meaning, "*I call upon you, Selene, ruler of the night, grant me intuition.*" Envision a silver sphere at your third eye, merging with a nocturnal seascape and awakening intuition. Unite with the Moon's acuity at the third eye.

Selene — lunar sovereignty, mistress of tides, dreams, and hidden currents — bestows the subtle receptivity to what lies beyond discursive reason: the direct, nocturnal gnosis that feels truths before they are voiced. This is the receptive complement to solar intellect necessary for a man who integrates polarities.

Sun: "**Καλέω σε, Ἥλιε, φωτὸς πηγὴν, δὸς μοι τὴν θεὶαν βούλησιν**" ("***Kaléō se, Hḗlie, phōtòs pēgèn, dòs moi tèn theían boúlēsin***"), meaning, ("*I call upon you, Helios, source of light, grant me divine will.*") Picture a golden sphere at your crown, standing in a radiant desert at noon, its heat igniting marvelous ingenuity. Imagine the Sun's radiance igniting the crown.

Helios — visible icon of intelligible Light and vast source of being and order — is summoned not for petty illumination or warmth, but the supreme gift of divine will itself. This is supra-personal volition descending from the Principle, an unerring orientation of soul toward what is eternal and necessary. It is the alignment of an individual center with the cosmic axis so complete that the personal will is annihilated in identity with the divine.

To invoke *Helios* is to demand a solar transfiguration: the one who receives no longer "wants" in the human, contingent sense; he becomes the vehicle of an impersonal, irresistible direction that burns away indecision, caprice, and the illusions of autonomy. It is the will that knows no hesitation because it is one with the very light that orders the worlds — virile, radiant, absolute.

This invocation crowns the ritual at a solar summit: after a preparatory fortification under planetary powers, following the adamantine integrity bestowed by the Morning Star, an initiate turns to the central luminary to receive the final, unifying gift. Endurance, preeminence, strength, integrity, agility, intuition, inspiration — all these subordinate qualities find their telos and justification here, in direct participation with divine volition that *Helios* mediates as the visible face of an invisible Principle.

Neptune: "**Καλέω σε, Ποσειδῶν, μυστικῶν ὑδάτων ἄρχοντα, δὸς μοι τὴν ἔμπνευσιν**" ("***Kaléō se, Poseidôn, mustikôn hudátōn árchonta, dòs moi tèn émpneusin***"), meaning, "*I call upon you, Poseidon, lord of mystic waters, grant me inspiration.*" Envision a violet sphere enveloping oneself in a misty ocean, evoking transcendent imagination. Encircle Neptune's deep purple glow around the entire body.

Poseidon, lord of the deeps, of seismic upheavals and a chthonic subliminal — his gift is the divine breath that surges from abyssal sources, the prophetic afflatus born of immersion in the primordial. Not superficial "creativity," but a vigorous, oceanic incursion that replenishes from the depths.

Conclude by picturing the eight energies merging within your subtle body along the vertical axis. Feel these dynamisms along your spine, activating an internal cosmos. Recite "**Ὡς ἄνω, οὕτως κάτω**" ("***Hōs ánō, hoútōs kátō***"), meaning, "*As above, so below.*"

The ritual's authenticity draws from the *Greek Magical Papyri's* invocatory style, where "**Καλέω σε**" summons heavenly powers, adapted here to focus on planetary forces. The altar serves as a hub for internal alignment and external orientation. Performed weekly, this cultivates lucidity (Neptune), virtuosity (Sun), insight (Moon), eloquence (Mercury), integrity (Venus), strength (Mars), nobility (Jupiter), and resolve (Saturn).

As a foundation for advanced workings, this prepares one for theurgic sacraments, thaumaturgic operations, or astral travel by establishing an equalized planetary structure. Regular practice supplements one's subtle physiology, embodying the concept of spiritual virility. To intensify the ritual, incorporate preparatory meditation on the *Pneuma*, visualizing breath as a luminous thread connecting the self to divinity.

The *Pneuma* is a divine breath linking one to the cosmic *Nous*. The ritual's breathing and recitations fortify this, infusing a subtle body with liveliness. Inner polarity balances active and receptive planetary forces, cultivating poise.

Thaumaturgic Manifestation and Theurgic Ascension

In Hermetic tradition, thaumaturgy and theurgy represent two interconnected facets of magical practice, each contributing to the practitioner's spiritual journey. Thaumaturgy, derived from the Greek for "wonder-working," involves practical magic to produce tangible effects in the physical world, such as healing, protection, or influencing natural forces. Theurgy, meaning "divine working," focuses on invoking higher intelligences (planetary spirits, divine archetypes, or cosmic principles) to achieve spiritual ascent and union with the divine.

Invocation and evocation are distinct methods of engaging with spiritual entities, each serving unique objectives in one's spiritual development. Invocation involves calling a spiritual being (deity, angel, or cosmic principle) into oneself, fostering an internal union that transubstantiates consciousness. This introspective process aspires to integrate the essence of an invoked entity, linking an individual with its power.

Evocation, by contrast, summons a spiritual entity to appear externally. This is often for purposes like gaining knowledge, receiving guidance, or achieving specific material outcomes. While invocation is unitive and transformative, evocation is interactive and often pragmatic, focusing on dialogue or assistance from a summoned entity.

This distinction is vividly illustrated in *The Greek Magical Papyri*. For instance, *PGM* IV.154-285 describes a ritual for invoking the god Osiris, where a practitioner seeks to merge with the deity's divine qualities, embodying its power and wisdom. This exemplifies invocation, as the objective is internal transformation. Conversely, *PGM* I.42-195 outlines an evocation ritual to summon a spirit for conversation, demonstrating an interaction where a practitioner seeks information or assistance. These texts highlight the Hermetic view of spiritual beings — such as angels, elementals, or deities — as manifestations of cosmic principles, serving as intermediaries between material and divine realms.

From an Evolian perspective, invocation holds a higher place in the hierarchy of magical practices, as it supports one's purpose of spiritual transcendence and realization of the Absolute Individual. In *The Hermetic Tradition*, Evola emphasizes the transformative power of internalizing divine qualities, interpreting invocation as a mechanism to transcend this material existence. Evocation, while potentially useful, is considered secondary unless it serves a higher spiritual goal, such as gaining insight to further one's ascent.

The historical roots of this distinction can be traced back to Neoplatonic philosophers like Iamblichus, who in *On the Mysteries* argued that theurgy, often involving invocation, unites one with the gods, surpassing human wisdom. This perspective influenced Hermeticism, which integrates Neoplatonic and medieval esoteric sources to present a cohesive system of spiritual transformation. An emphasis on invocation aligns with the aim of attaining *Henosis*, or union with the divine, predominantly through internal revelation rather than external spectacle.

Thaumaturgy is magic aimed at producing tangible effects in the physical world, such as healing, protection, or influencing natural forces. In the Hermetic tradition, thaumaturgy is not merely about achieving practical outcomes but serves as a preparatory stage for higher spiritual work. Evola describes thaumaturgical practices as methods to master external forces, thereby disciplining a practitioner's will and preparing them for the deeper spiritual demands of theurgy.

For example, the ritual of "Instructions for Magical Chains" involves creating a symbolic link among practitioners to amplify their collective energy, enhancing spiritual focus and power. This practice, rooted in the principle of correspondence ("as above, so below"), demonstrates how thaumaturgical acts bridge the material and spiritual realms.

Similarly, the "Magic of Effigies" uses physical depictions to influence material consequences, grounding one in an interplay between microcosm (individual) and macrocosm (the universe). These acts are not ends in themselves, but tools to purify and strengthen the practitioner.

Thaumaturgy's role extends beyond practicality. In the context of the Golden Dawn, a 19th-century magical order, it was integrated into a structured curriculum combining rituals for material effects with spiritual exercises. This historical context underscores thaumaturgy's versatility, as it was commissioned for purposes ranging from healing to invoking spirits. Evola's interpretation builds on this tradition, viewing thaumaturgy as a foundation for theurgy, where mastery of external forces cultivates discipline and clarity needed for spiritual ascent.

In *The Hermetic Tradition*, Evola investigates thaumaturgy within the framework of alchemy, presenting it as a universal science of transformation. Alchemical practices — such as the manipulation of metals or construction of talismans — are thaumaturgical in nature, involving actions to influence the material world. However, Evola maintains that these acts are metaphysical, serving as a bridge to the spiritual transformation central to theurgy. This perspective aligns with the Hermetic view that all magical implementations are interconnected, reflecting the principle of correspondence.

Theurgy is the practice of invoking and internalizing higher intelligences to achieve spiritual ascent and union with the divine. Unlike thaumaturgy's application toward external effects, theurgy emphasizes internal transformation, where contact with the divine is experienced as a felt presence or internal insight, rather than necessarily as an external apparition.

In the *Corpus Hermeticum*, particularly in the *Poimandres*, Hermes Trismegistus receives a vision from *Nous*, the Divine Mind, imparting knowledge of the cosmos and the path to salvation. This internal revelation transforms the practitioner's understanding, imparting profound wisdom.

Evola frames theurgy as the pinnacle of magical practice, akin to the alchemical Great Work, wherein one undergoes a symbolic and metaphysical transformation to realize the self as a divine entity. Theurgy is a procedure involving prayer, meditation, and ritual that surpasses ordinary intellect to ascend through the layers of being. The Neoplatonist Proclus described theurgy as a power embracing divine possession. In the Hermetic context, theurgy is a passageway to immortality, achieving *Henosis* through spiritual rebirth and ascension.

Theurgic practices often involve silence and contemplation, as noted in the *Definitions of Hermes Trismegistus to Asclepius*, where silence is key to receiving divine power. This emphasis on inner receptivity resonates an outlook prioritizing spiritual discipline and transcendence of material concerns. Theurgy is a way of life where one strives to realize the Absolute Individual — a state of spiritual sovereignty.

Thaumaturgy and theurgy share several components in the Hermetic tradition, reflecting a unity of magical practice. Both rely on the principle of correspondence, where actions in the material world mirror and influence the spiritual realm. Rituals create a sacred space bridging a practitioner and the deific, often involving divine names, emblematic implements like sigils or talismans, and effective ceremonies.

In thaumaturgy, charged symbols like an octagram or planetary signatures influence material outcomes, as seen in effigy creation or rituals affecting natural energies. In theurgy, these symbols harmonize one with deific dynamisms, facilitating spiritual ascent. In the *Asclepius*, rituals use divine names and symbols to invoke higher powers, reflecting an interconnectedness of practical and spiritual magic. This emphasizes how these combined elements (symbols, rituals, and divine names) form a cohesive system where thaumaturgy prepares the ground for theurgy.

Divine names are particularly powerful, acting as vibrational keys resonating with higher forces. In *The Greek Magical Papyri*, names like *IAO* or *Abrasax* harness metaphysical power for both thaumaturgical and theurgic objectives. Neoplatonic philosophy underscores their importance in enabling one to ally with divine order, reflecting the Hermetic view that all magical practices are part of a cohesive path toward transformation.

In Hermetic philosophy, the human being is a microcosm of the universe, comprising soul (*Nous*), spirit (*Pneuma*), and body (*Soma*). These correspond to the alchemical primes — Sulfur, Mercury, and Salt — fundamental principles representing essential components of all life. Sulfur, associated with the soul, embodies an active, fiery principle of awareness, corresponding to *Nous*, the divine mind and source of intelligence. Mercury, or quicksilver, represents spirit, signifying fluidity and mediation between realms, akin to *Pneuma*, the vital breath connecting physical and spiritual. Salt signifies the body, representing fixity and stability, analogous to *Soma*, the physical vessel for divine work.

This integration of alchemical primes into the Hermetic triad creates a comprehensive framework bridging material and spiritual dimensions. Sulfur (*θεῖον*) ignites the divine spark within, Mercury (*ὕδραργυρος*) facilitates the flow of divine essence, and Salt (*ἅλας*) grounds a practitioner in the material world. By invoking these correspondences, one aligns with the universal order, reflecting the Hermetic maxim "as above, so below." This orientation enhances the spiritual significance of a ritual, facilitating transformation and ascension.

Invoking the Triad with Alchemical Primes

The following ritual invokes *Nous*, *Pneuma*, and *Soma*, integrated with their alchemical counterparts — Sulfur, Mercury, and Salt — to harmonize these aspects within. This practice draws from Hermetic texts.

To perform this invocation effectively, a practitioner should prepare a sacred space conducive to spiritual focus. A quiet, dimly lit room minimizes distractions, and a small altar can be adorned with symbols such as an octagram, representing the microcosm-macrocosm connection, or a circle divided into three parts to symbolize *Nous* (Sulfur), *Pneuma* (Mercury), and *Soma* (Salt). These visual cues support the Hermetic principle of correspondence, facilitating a connection between the practitioner and the divine.

Frankincense, noted in the *Asclepius* for its purifying qualities, should be used to create a sacred atmosphere, cleansing the space of negative energies. A candle or oil lamp can symbolize the light of *Nous*, enhancing a ritual's focus on divine illumination. Preparation should include meditation or fasting to purify the mind and body. A cleansing ritual, such as an ablution done while reciting a purifying prayer, may precede the invocation to enhance receptivity.

The invocation should be recited slowly and with intention, with a practitioner visualizing the fiery Sulfur of *Nous* illuminating their consciousness, the fluid Mercury of *Pneuma* rousing their lifeforce, and the stable Salt of Soma grounding their physical form. The Greek is utilized for authenticity and pronounced with awe to boost effectiveness. The practitioner should focus on the sensation of these aspects uniting within them, fostering harmony and spiritual alignment.

The ritual is best performed at dawn, facing the rising sun, to symbolize the awakening of divine knowledge, associating with the prominence of sunlight as a Hermetic metaphor for wisdom. The invocation should be integrated into a regular practice, such as weekly rituals, to foster a sustained connection with the divine triad and alchemical primes. Practitioners should reflect on any insights or sensations experienced during the ritual, as these may indicate an internal presence of invoked aspects.

Invocation

Ἐπικαλοῦμαι τὸ Θεῖον Νοῦν, Ψυχήν, πηγὴν πάσης σοφίας καὶ φωτός, ἵνα φωτίσῃ τὸν νοῦν μου καὶ ὁδηγήσῃ τὰς σκέψεις μου πρὸς τὴν αἰώνιον ἀλήθειαν.

Ἐπικαλοῦμαι τὴν Ἱερὰν Πνεῦμα, Ψυχήν, ὑδράργυρον πνοὴν ζωῆς, ἵνα ζωογονήσῃ τὸ εἶναί μου

καὶ συνδέσῃ με μετὰ τῆς θείας οὐσίας τῆς ῥεούσης διὰ πάσης τῆς κτίσεως.

Ἐπικαλοῦμαι τὸ Ἅγιον Σῶμα, Σῶμα, ἅλα τῆς γῆς καὶ σκεῦος τῆς ὑπάρξεώς μου, ἵνα καθαρισθῇ καὶ ἐνισχυθῇ, ὑπηρετοῦν ὡς ναὸς τοῦ θείου.

Ἅμα, ἔστω τὸ θεῖον τοῦ Νοῦς, ὁ ὑδράργυρος τοῦ Πνεύματος, καὶ τὸ ἅλας τοῦ Σώματος ἑνωμένα ἐν ἐμοί, ὥστε βαδίσαι τὴν ὁδὸν τῆς Ἑρμητικῆς σοφίας, ἐπιτυγχάνοντα ἁρμονίαν καὶ ἀνάβασιν ἐν πνεύματι, ψυχῇ, καὶ σώματι.

Epikaloumài tò Theîon Noûn, Psuchḗn, pēgḕn pásēs sophías kaì phōtós, hína phōtísēi tòn noûn mou kaì hodēgḗsēi tàs sképseis mou pròs tḕn aiṓnion alḗtheian.

Epikaloumài tḕn Hieràn Pneûma, Psuchḗn, hudrárgyron pnoḕn zōês, hína zōogonḗsēi tò eînai mou kaì sundésēi me metà tês theías ousías tês rheoúsēs dià pásēs tês ktíseōs.

Epikaloumài tò Hágion Sôma, Sôma, hála tês gês kaì skeûos tês hupárxeōs mou, hína katharisthêi kaì enischuthêi, huperetoûn hōs naòs toû theíou.

Háma, éstō tò theîon toû Noûs, ho hudrárgyros toû Pneúmatos, kaì tò hála toû Sṓmatos henōmena en emoí, hṓste badísai tḕn hodòn tês Hermētikês sophías, epitynchánonta harmonían kaì anábasin en pneúmati, psuchêi, kaì sṓmati.

"I invoke the Divine Soul, Nous, source of all wisdom and light, to illuminate my mind and guide my thoughts toward the eternal truth.

"I invoke the Sacred Spirit, Pneuma, mercurial breath of life, to animate my being and connect me to the divine essence flowing through all creation.

"I invoke the Holy Body, Soma, Salt of the earth and vessel of my existence, to be purified and strengthened, serving as a temple for the divine.

"Together, may the Sulfur of the Soul, the Mercury of the Spirit, and the Salt of the Body be united within me, that I may walk the path of Hermetic wisdom, achieving harmony and ascension in spirit, soul, and body."

Integrating Sulfur, Mercury, and Salt into the Hermetic triad reflects an alchemical principle of the *Tria Prima*, where these primes are building blocks of all creation. Sulfur's fiery nature aligns with *Nous's* divine spark, Mercury's fluidity mirrors *Pneuma's* mediating role, and Salt's stability links to *Soma's* material foundation. Established in Paracelsus's instruction, this correspondence enhances a ritual's transformative power, joining one with the spiritual order.

Evola's philosophy emphasizes the transformative potency of spiritual trainings like theurgy, counteracting a degeneration of modern society. By summoning *Nous* (Sulfur), *Pneuma* (Mercury), and *Soma* (Salt) in a microcosmic deed supporting the macrocosmic order, an individual acts as a potential vessel for divine realization.

This ritual mirrors the alchemical process where one undergoes a symbolic metamorphosis akin to transmuting base metals into gold, achieving spiritual ascension and realizing the Absolute Individual.

Thaumaturgy and theurgy are integral to the Hermetic path, with the former giving a concrete foundation to the latter's higher aspirations. The difference between invocation and evocation show internal and external approaches to dealing with spiritual entities, with invocation as central to alteration. The shared components of symbol, ritual, and divine names stress a unity of these practices.

The ceremony invoking *Nous* (Sulfur), *Pneuma* (Mercury), and *Soma* (Salt) offers a practical tool to harmonize these properties, forming a bond with superior energies and actualizing a spiritual existence. Through controlled routine, a practitioner can embody powerful cosmic dynamisms in line with Evola's vision of spiritual transcendence.

The Magic of Effigies

The Magic of Effigies is a potent esoteric device employing physical representations to influence material outcomes. This practice is based in an interplay between microcosm (individual) and macrocosm (universe), a cornerstone of Hermeticism. It offers a powerful method to use on one's quest for spiritual discipline and self-realization.

The Magic of Effigies rests on the Hermetic principle of correspondence: "That which is below is like that which is above, and that which is above is like that which is below, to perform the miracles of one thing." This axiom declares that a person (microcosm) reflects material reality (macrocosm), enabling one to effect tangible changes in existence by manipulating a smaller representation. The effigy, as a simulacrum, becomes a bridge between these realms, channeling a practitioner's intent into the objective world.

This practice is a means of mastering external forces through disciplined will. The effigy is not a passive object but a vessel for spiritual energy ("fluid"), which an operator activates through ritual. This aligns with Hermetic philosophy's view that the universe is a mental construct responsive to focused intent, underscoring the technique's potential efficacy.

Effigies have been used across cultures, from ancient Egyptian *ushabti* figures believed to serve the deceased in the afterlife, to medieval European poppets in sympathetic magic. An adaptation of the Magic of Effigies builds on this legacy, emphasizing its actual application within a metaphysical framework.

To Evola, magic is for transcending material limitations and achieving spiritual sovereignty. Practices like the Magic of Effigies train a practitioner to align their will with the macrocosm, fostering an actualized spiritual existence. This is not about petty desires, but refining self through interaction with the cosmos, a process demanding integrity and reverence.

The Magic of Effigies Ritual

Below is a detailed adaptation of the Magic of Effigies ritual, integrating Hermetic components and Greek language/characters. This ritual is designed to influence a specific material outcome — such as recovery, protection, or power — while progressing the practitioner's spiritual growth.

Cleansing the Space

Purify the ritual area with frankincense, routine in Hermetic rites for its cleansing properties. As you light the incense, recite:

Καθαρίζω τὸν χῶρον τοῦτον, ἵνα ἁγνὸς ᾖ πρὸς τὸ ἔργον τῆς μαγείας.

Katharízō tòn chō̃ron toûton, hína hagnòs êi pròs tò érgon tês mageías.

"I cleanse this space, that it may be pure for the work of magic."

Mental Preparation

Sit in silence, meditating for 8-12 minutes to clear your mind. Visualize the desired outcome, holding this intention firmly as you proceed.

Creation of the Effigy

Choose a medium aligned with your intent: clay for healing, wax for protection, wood for power. The material should resonate symbolically with the goal. Shape it into a small figure representing the recipient (a person, object, or concept). Focus your will into the effigy as you form it.

Inscribe it with Greek letters or Hermetic symbols tied to the intent: *healing* ("**ΥΓΙΕΙΑ**" — ***"Ygieia"***), *protection* ("**ΦΥΛΑΞΙΣ**" — ***"Fylaxis"***), and *power* ("**Δ'ΥΝΑΜΗ**" — ***"Dýnami"***).

Optionally, add symbols like the Caduceus (☤) to enhance a connection to the Hermetic patron, Thrice-Great.

Invocation

Invoke Hermes Trismegistus, Hermetic archetype of divine mediation, by raising your hands and saying:

Εἰς τὸν Ἑρμῆν τὸν Τρισμέγιστον, τὸν ὁδηγὸν τῆς σοφίας καὶ τὸν κήρυκα τῶν θεῶν, κράζω. Ἔλθοι μοι, ὦ Ἑρμῆ, καὶ ἐνίσχυσον τὸ ἔργον τοῦτο.

Eis tòn Hermên tòn Trismégiston, tòn hodēgòn tês sophías kaì tòn kêruka tôn theôn, krázō. Élthoi moi, ō Hermê, kaì eníschuson tò érgon toûto.

"To Hermes the Thrice-Greatest, guide of wisdom and herald of the gods, I call. Come to me, O Hermes, and empower this work."

Address the effigy directly, stating its purpose:

Ὦ εἴδωλον, σὺ εἶ τὸ σῶμα, καὶ διὰ σοῦ ἐπιδρῶ εἰς τὸν κόσμον.

Ō eídōlon, sù eî tò sôma, kaì dià soû epidrô eis tòn kósmon.

"O effigy, you are the body, and through you I act upon the world."

Close your eyes and envision golden light descending from the cosmos, flowing through you into the effigy. See it radiate with this energy.

Amplify the energy by chanting three times:

Δύναμις τοῦ κόσμου, ῥεῖ δι' ἐμοῦ, εἰς τὸ εἴδωλον.

Dúnamis toû kósmou, rheî di' emoû, eis tò eídōlon.

"Power of the cosmos, flow through me, into the effigy."

Activate the effigy with an action tied to the intent: anoint with oil for healing, encircle with Salt for protection, or light a candle for empowerment.

Conclude by sealing the work:

Τὸ ἔργον τετέλεσται. Ἐν τῷ ὀνόματι τοῦ Ἑρμοῦ, σφραγίζω τὴν μαγείαν ταύτην.

Tò érgon tetélestai. En tôi onómati toû Hermoû, sphragízō tèn mageían taútēn.

"The work is complete. In the name of Hermes, I seal this magic."

Keep the effigy in a sacred space, bury it, or destroy it (e.g., by burning), depending on the intent (retain for ongoing effects or dispose for banishment).

The Magic of Effigies should not serve corrupted ends, but harmonize with one's highest aspiration, reflecting the Hermetic ideal of theurgy: divine work that elevates the soul. Practitioners must approach it with reverence, ensuring their intent supports personal and universal growth.

The Magic of Effigies blends practical efficacy with spiritual depth. By engaging the interplay of personal and cosmic, it enables one to shape reality while advancing toward apotheosis.

The Power of Collective Practice

As articulated in *Introduction to Magic, Vol. I: Rituals and Practical Techniques for the Magus*, the concept of a "magical chain" represents a profound method for amplifying spiritual power through collective practice. A group of individuals, through synchronized rituals and shared intention, generates a spiritual force greater than the sum of individual efforts. This power, referred to as "collective force," is a real thing: a coagulation of astral light harnessed for purposes such as illumination, practical outcomes, or initiation of neophytes. The group's unified will enables powerful transformative effects on both material and spiritual planes.

Evola's philosophy frames the magical chain as a tool for attaining spiritual dominion. The practice transcends mere collaboration, creating a hierarchical structure where a leader, recognized for their spiritual dignity, guides the group. This order — whether inherited, developed, or conferred — ensures the collective force is directed purposefully in concert with a ranked social organization conforming to Traditional principles.

Historically, the UR Group (formed in 1927 by Evola and other Italian esotericists) aimed to develop transcendent forces through such practices. Their success was notable, as evidenced by rumors of their power spreading through Italy, even causing concern for Mussolini. The magical chain, as practiced by the UR Group, involved rigorous timing, shared symbols, and rituals, often performed simultaneously by members, whether together or apart, to create a unified spiritual entity.

Forming a magical group in today's world requires careful planning, especially given the potential for geographical separation and varying circumstances among members. The process involves selecting suitable participants, establishing shared goals, and leveraging technology for coordination.

Selecting Members

Choose individuals who are committed to spiritual growth and share a common understanding of the group's objectives. Members should have a foundational knowledge of esoteric practices, such as meditation or ritual work, to ensure coherence in group operations.

Qualities like reliability, integrity, and a capacity to operate amicably are beyond indispensable. In a contemporary context, associates can be found through online esoteric communities, local spiritual and corresponding interest groups (meditation, yoga, martial arts, philosophical discussion, etc.), or personal networks. In any milieu, careful vetting is necessary to ensure alignment with the group's purpose.

The order must define its commitment clearly, whether it is spiritual development, practical magic, or an amalgamation of both. Agree on specific rituals, texts, and symbols to be used, drawing from Hermetic traditions or other esoteric sources relevant to the group's focus. For example, the assembly might adopt a sigil or symbol (such as a Caduceus) representing their collective intention. Create a plan for synchronized operations, accounting for time zones if necessary. Regular virtual meetings via online discussion or conferencing platforms can facilitate planning and comradery.

Present-day technology enables groups to function effectively despite physical distance. Use video calls, messaging apps, or online forums for regular communication, sharing experiences, and addressing issues. Create a shared digital space such as a private chatroom or website to distribute ritual scripts, schedules, and resources. For virtual rituals, ensure all members have the basic materials (e.g., candles, incense, symbols) and understand the procedures. Coordinated timing is critical, so use tools like world clocks or notifications to coordinate simultaneous commencement.

However, if possible, in-person group work and interaction is preferable to at-distance. This is why utilizing resident sources of recruitment should at least be investigated. Conversely, persons especially committed to an esoteric order may travel distances to congregate and practice. These semi-regular gatherings could be supplemented with virtual fellowship and procedures to solidify the bond and efficacy of a group when locations differ.

Collective practice can face several challenges, which must be addressed to maintain the integrity of the magical chain:

Ego Clashes: Differences in experience or interpretation can lead to disagreements. Foster a culture of humility and mutual respect, emphasizing a group's collective goals over individual agendas. Regular discussions and a clear leadership structure can help mediate conflicts.

Adverse Intent: Negative energies or misaligned intentions can disrupt the group's congruence. Screen potential members carefully, assessing their motivations and commitment. If issues surface, address them punctually through open dialogue or, if necessary, by removing disruptive individuals.

Malevolent or Underhanded Behavior: Treacherous actions undermine trust and the group's spiritual integrity. Implement a zero-tolerance policy for harmful behavior, with mechanisms to detect and expel members who engage in duplicity or malice. Consistent group deliberations can help recognize and confront such issues by bringing them into the open.

To ensure group cohesion, hold routine meetings to discuss progress and resolve conflicts. Communal meditations or energy alignment sessions can strengthen the collective bond. Rituals designed to underpin the group's coherence, such as collective visualizations or chants, can enhance syntony; the harmonious alignment of energies is essential for a magical chain. A leader with recognized spiritual authority should guide the group, ensuring focus and discipline while fostering an milieu of mutual support.

To contribute effectively to the magical chain, each member must engage in individual practices that enhance their spiritual readiness and align their energies with the group's purpose. These preparations strengthen personal discipline and ensure the collective force is potent and cohesive.

Meditate on the group's chosen symbol (e.g., octagram with a planetary sigil of Mercury at its center) daily to internalize its significance, furthering syntony within the group. Spend time visualizing the shared intention to align personal energy with a collective awareness. These practices strengthen focus, enhance discipline, and cultivate a communal spiritual bond.

Anoint with oils to cleanse the body and aura before group operations. Avoid substantial foods on ritual days to maintain physical and mental clarity. Burn incense to purify the personal space, in line with the Hermetic tradition's emphasis on spiritual hygiene.

Recite affirmations related to the group's goal, such as "I am aligned with the divine purpose of our chain," to reinforce commitment. Document dreams, synchronicities, or intuitions related to the group's work to deepen a personal connection to the collective intention.

Pre-ritual preparations ensure members and their spaces are spiritually aligned, enhancing the efficacy of a collective ritual. Take a bath with sea salt and oil to cleanse the body and aura, preparing for spiritual work. Fast a few hours before the ritual to maintain mental clarity and physical lightness.

Space Cleansing: Ensure the area is clean, quiet, and absent distractions, creating a conducive environment for focus.

Orientation: Position the altar and participants facing north, invoking a Hyperborean orientation and vertical polarity.

Altar Setup: Prepare an altar ornamented with a candle (symbolizing illumination), chalice of water (for reflection), incense, and the group's shared symbol.

Incense Purification: Burn frankincense or other traditional Hermetic incenses to purify the space of negative energies.

Meditation: Meditate for 8-12 minutes to center the mind and focus on the ritual's purpose.

Breathing Exercises: Perform deep breathing exercises, such as diaphragmatic breathing, to calm the nervous system and enhance concentration.

Personal Invocation: Recite a brief personal prayer, such as "I align my will with the divine and our collective purpose," to prepare emotionally and spiritually.

The Collective Ritual: A Hermetic Magical Chain

The following ritual is designed to create a magical chain, empowering both individual members and the group as a whole. It draws upon traditions, featuring the Prayer of Thanksgiving from the *Greek Magical Papyri* and *Corpus Hermeticum*. The ritual is structured to be performed simultaneously by all members, whether physically together or virtually, to maximize the collective magical force.

Light the candle and incense, symbolizing divine light and purification. Sprinkle a few drops of water from the bowl around the altar, saying:

Καθαρίζω τὸν χῶρον τοῦτον, ἵνα ἁγνὸς ᾖ πρὸς τὸ ἔργον τῆς μαγείας.

Katharízō tòn chō̃ron toûton, hína hagnòs êi pròs tò érgon tês mageías.

"I cleanse this space, that it may be pure for the work of magic."

Take three deep breaths, focusing on the shared intention.

Invocation of the Divine

Stand facing north, raising hands to the sky, and recite the Hermetic Prayer of Thanksgiving to invoke a divine connection:

Εὐχαριστοῦμεν σοι, ὦ ἄρρητε ὄνομα, τὸ τιμώμενον ὡς θεός, τὸ αἰνούμενον ὡς πατήρ, ὅτι πᾶσιν καὶ πᾶσιν ἔδειξας πατρικὴν εὐσέβειαν, φιλίαν, ἀγάπην, καὶ γλυκυτάτην ἐνέργειαν, δωρούμενος ἡμῖν νοῦν, λόγον, γνῶσιν: νοῦν, ἵνα σε καταλάβωμεν· λόγον, ἵνα σε ἐπικαλεσώμεθα· γνῶσιν, ἵνα σε γνῶμεν.

Eucharistoûmen soi, ō árrēte ónoma, tò timṓmenon hōs theós, tò ainóumenon hōs patḕr, hóti pâsin kaì pâsin édeixas patrikḕn eusébeian, philían, agápen, kaì glukutátēn enérgeian, dōroúmenos hēmîn noûn, lógon, gnôsin: noûn, hína se katalábōmen; lógon, hína se epikalesṓmetha; gnôsin, hína se gnômen.

"We give thanks to you, o ineffable Name, honored as God and praised as Father, for to everyone and everything you have shown fatherly kindness, affection, love, and sweetest activity, granting to us mind, word, and knowledge: mind, that we may understand you; word, that we may call upon you; knowledge, that we may know you."

This prayer, found in *PGM III.591-611* and the *Asclepius*, connects with divine wisdom, fostering spiritual elevation.

Formation of the Magical Chain

Visualize a light emanating from your heart and connecting to the hearts of all a part of the group, forming an illuminated tether connected to each member, now enveloped in radiance.

Chant the seven Greek vowels (**Α Ε Η Ι Ο Υ Ω** — "*Ah, Eh, Ay, Ee, Oh, Oo, Aw*") three times, slowly and regularly, to raise vibrational energy and enhance syntony. Used in Hermetic cosmology, these vowels correspond to the main planetary spheres, amplifying the group's cosmic resonance.

Focus on the group's shared symbol, visualizing it glowing with the collective energy, becoming a focal point for the magical chain.

Affirmation of Collective Intention

Each member states the group's intention aloud, in unison if possible, or sequentially in a virtual setting: "We unite our wills to achieve [state specific goal]."

Examples of goals include "illumination," "protection," or "healing." The statement should be concise and aligned with the group's purpose.

Empowerment and Circulation of Energy

Visualize the golden light circulating throughout the chain, empowering each member and strengthening the cooperative force.

Chant the following to amplify the energy:

Δύναμις τοῦ κόσμου, ῥεῖ δι' ἡμῶν, ἑνοῦσα τὰς ψυχὰς ἡμῶν.

Dúnamis toû kósmou, rheî di' hēmôn, henoûsa tàs psuchàs hēmôn.

"Power of the cosmos, flow through us, uniting our souls."

Repeat this chant three times, feeling the energy build and connect the group.

Closing and Grounding

Thank the divine with a final prayer:

Εὐχαριστοῦμεν τῷ θείῳ ὀνόματι διὰ τὴν ἑνότητα καὶ τὴν δύναμιν ἡμῶν.

Eucharistoûmen tôi theíōi onómati dià tèn henótēta kaì tèn dúnamin hēmôn.

"We thank the divine Name for our unity and power."

Extinguish the candle and incense, symbolizing completion of the ritual. Ground yourself by touching the earth, drinking water and eating a snack to return to normal consciousness. If virtual, members should share experiences via a group chat or call to reinforce the collective bond.

Practical Considerations

Ensure all members have the ritual script, including Greek pronunciations (e.g., "**Εὐχαριστοῦμεν**" is pronounced "*Ef-kha-ree-stoo-men*"). Practice the Greek text for fluency. Use a clock or group signal (e.g., message in a chat) to start simultaneously. This is critical for virtual rituals.

Each member needs a candle, incense, and the group symbol (ensure figurative consistency). Share experiences and insights in a discussion to deepen the collective connection and assess the ritual's impact. Perform rituals after the new moon and prior to full moons to maintain a magical chain's strength, adjusting intentions as necessary.

Evola's philosophy emphasizes spiritual discipline and transcendence of material limitations. The magical chain aligns with this by uniting individual wills into a collective force that resonates with cosmic principles, fostering the realization of the Absolute Individual. The ritual's use of Hermetic elements, such as the Prayer of Thanksgiving and Greek vowels, connects it to the ancient wisdom traditions, while its focus on empowerment reflects his vision of spiritual sovereignty.

The magical chain was a central UR Group practice, with a documented instance in 1928 involving a Genoa group of five, linked by a chain established by a Rome director. This historical precedent underscores an efficacy of synchronized ritual, even across distances (a pertinent attitude for virtual groups).

Ensure all members perform identical practices — such as chanting the same vowels or focusing on the same symbol — to achieve energetic harmony. Appoint a leader with spiritual authority to guide the ritual, ensuring focus and discipline. Consistent rituals strengthen the chain, making it a living entity that perpetuates a group's spiritual tradition.

The magical chain, as articulated by Evola and the UR Group, is a powerful practice for amplifying spiritual energy through collective effort. By forming a discipline, addressing pitfalls, and preparing both individually and collectively, practitioners can harness this force for spiritual and practical outcomes.

The Hermetic ritual provided, with its Greek invocations and synchronized actions, sanctions both individuals and the group. Through consistent practice and commitment, the magical chain becomes a transformative tool for actualized spiritual existence.

Advanced Techniques for Higher Consciousness

The pursuit of superior perception surpasses paltry intellectual speculation. It is more so a fundamentally transformational journey toward spiritual self-government and personal realization. Thus, Evola's philosophy positions certain skills as pinnacle techniques for transcending the material self and accessing higher states.

Trance is described as an altered state of consciousness that pierces the veil of ordinary perception, granting spiritual insight and inner power. Far from a passive or hypnotic condition, it is an active, disciplined state cultivated through intent and practice. *Ekstasis*, a term meaning "standing outside oneself," elevates this further into a divine ecstasy — a union with the transcendent that mirrors the Hermetic ideal of *Henosis*, or oneness with the divine.

These states are not ends in themselves, but junctures of an alchemical opus. In *The Hermetic Tradition*, Evola frames this as a metaphysical process where one refines their base, profane nature into a divine essence, akin to transforming lead into gold. This is not a metaphor but a lived reality, requiring one to engage with these techniques as acts of spiritual warfare against the limitations of the mundane.

Evola's warnings in *Introduction to Magic, Vol. III* underscore the risks of these practices: without proper preparation, trance and *ekstasis* can destabilize the intellect or exhaust the body, leading to psychological fragmentation or physical breakdown. Safety hinges on a triad of prerequisites.

Purification: Cleansing the body and spirit through fasting, ritual baths, and abstaining from impurities removes obstacles to deific connection.

Meditation: Honed through consistent meditative practice, a disciplined mind ensures focus and resilience during altered states.

Ethical Control: Virtues such as openness, honesty, courage, and detachment from physical desires fortify a practitioner's inner stability.

These steps echo the Hermetic maxim "know thyself," preparing an individual to embrace the godlike without being overcome by it. A stable location — quiet, free of interruptions — is equally critical, as external chaos can disrupt the delicate balance of these states.

Hermetic Ritual for Trance and *Ekstasis*

Designed for solitary use (though adaptable for groups), this ritual guides one through a structure of purification, invocation, and ascent into trance culminating in *ekstasis*.

Preparation

Prepare a quiet, dimly lit room free from distractions. Orient the space northward. Perform the ritual at midnight, a potent moment in Hermetic cosmology tapping into the chasm of the subconscious. Wear a white robe, signifying purity and heavenly radiance (avoid synthetic fabrics as natural materials like cotton or linen enhance energetic flow).

Construct a small altar equipped with a white pillar candle (symbolizing illumination), bowl of water (for purification and reflection), small mirror (representing self-awareness), and Caduceus or image of Hermes Trismegistus (guide of souls).

Take a ritual bath with sea salt and oil, cleansing body and aura. Fast for at least three hours prior to heighten sensitivity and focus.

Ritual Performance

Light the candle and frankincense, filling the space with their purifying substance. Stand before the altar, take three deep breaths (inhale through the nose, exhale through the mouth), and visualize roots extending from your feet into the earth, anchoring you. Recite:

Καθαρίζω τὸν χῶρον καὶ τὸν ἑαυτόν μου, ἵνα ἁγνὸς ᾖ πρὸς τὸ ἔργον τῆς μαγείας.

Katharízō tòn chō̃ron kaì tòn heautón mou, hína hagnòs êi pròs tò érgon tês mageías.

"I cleanse this space and myself, that I may be pure for the work of magic."

Feel the weight of impurities lifting, leaving you clear and grounded.

Raise your hands, palms upward, and invoke Hermes, the psychopomp and mediator of divine wisdom:

Εἰς τὸν Ἑρμῆν τὸν Τρισμέγιστον, τὸν ὁδηγὸν τῆς σοφίας καὶ τὸν κῆρυκα τῶν θεῶν, κράζω. Ἔλθοι μοι, ὦ Ἑρμῆ, καὶ ὁδήγησόν με εἰς τὴν ἔκστασιν.

Eis tòn Hermên tòn Trismégiston, tòn hodēgòn tês sophías kaì tòn kêruka tôn theôn, krázō. Élthoi moi, ō Hermê, kaì hodḗgēsón me eis tèn ékstasin.

"To Hermes the Thrice-Greatest, guide of wisdom and herald of the gods, I call. Come to me, O Hermes, and lead me into ekstasis."

Visualize Hermes appearing before you, cloaked in shimmering light and holding the Caduceus. Sense his presence as a passage between the mortal and divine realms.

Sit comfortably (cross-legged or on a chair), close your eyes, and begin a 4-4-4-4 breathing pattern: inhale for four counts, hold for four, exhale for four, hold for four.

Repeat for 4-8 minutes, letting each breath deepen your relaxation. Feel your body soften and your mind quiet, slipping into a light trance as thoughts dissolve.

Chant the seven Greek vowels, each linked to a planetary sphere in the Hermetic cosmology: A (*Alpha*) — Earth/Moon, E (*Epsilon*) — Mercury, H (*Eta*) — Venus, I (*Iota*) — Sun, O (*Omicron*) — Mars, Y (*Upsilon*) — Jupiter, Ω (*Omega*) — Saturn.

Pronounce each vowel slowly, feeling its deep resonance vibrate through your chest and skull. Repeat the sequence three times, visualizing your energy field expanding outward with each cycle.

Imagine a golden ladder or staircase rising through the seven planetary spheres. With each step, shed an aspect of your lower self: emotional attachments for *Luna*, disparate thoughts for *Mercurius*, sensual fixations for *Venus*, egocentricity for *Sol*, hyper-aggression for *Mars*, trifling ambition for *Jupiter*, limitations and scarcity for *Saturnus*. At the summit, see a bright, boundless light (the Divine Source) beckoning you upward.

As you reach the light surrender your lower self, merging into our true identity as Higher Mind. Feel your consciousness expand beyond your body, becoming pure awareness. Recite:

Ἐγὼ εἰμι τὸ φῶς, ἐγὼ εἰμι τὸ πνεῦμα, ἐγὼ εἰμι τὸ ἕν.

Egȍ eimi tò phôs, egȍ eimi tò pneûma, egȍ eimi tò hén.

"I am the light, I am the spirit, I am the One."

Linger in this state — open to visions, intuitions, or a sense of gravity — for as long as feels natural. Slowly descend the ladder, reintegrating the purified aspects of yourself into being. Visualize your awareness settling back into your body, rooted to the earth.

Open your eyes, take a deep breath, and drink from the bowl of water to anchor yourself. Offer gratitude, reciting:

Εὐχαριστῶ τῷ Ἑρμῇ καὶ τῷ θείῳ ὀνόματι διὰ τὴν ἔκστασιν καὶ τὴν σοφίαν.

Eucharistô tôi Hermêi kaì tôi theíōi onómati dià tḕn ékstasin kaì tḕn sophían.

"I thank Hermes and the divine Name for the ekstasis and wisdom."

Extinguish the candle and incense, marking the ritual's close.

Post-Ritual Reflection

Record your experiences in a journal by noting sensations, visions, or revelations. Reflect on how this practice has shifted your perception and consider integrating its lessons into daily life — perhaps through continued meditation or refinement.

As advanced techniques for higher consciousness, trance and *ekstasis* demonstrate active transcendence. Grounded in preparation and executed with reverence, the ritual outlined offers a means to explore these conditions. Regular engagement with such techniques can progressively unveil the divine within, fulfilling the alchemical promise of self-transformation.

Trial of the Threshold

The Trial of the Threshold marks a critical juncture in the initiatic journey. It is a moment wherein one faces the daemonic double, the Threshold Guardian, in a test of spiritual resolve and purity. Explored in *Introduction to Magic, Vol. I*, this procedure surpasses metaphor, offering a real encounter with an entity guarding the passage from mundane to sacred.

In the UR Group's framework, the daemonic double is not a fleeting psychological shadow, but a tangible astral presence embodying one's unresolved energies: fears, desires, and inner conflicts. It emerges as a formidable adversary during the Trial, challenging one's readiness to ascend to higher states of being.

This entity materializes in one's *eidolon* as an ethereal twin reflecting a soul's dual potential for ascent or descent. In Greek tradition, the *daemon* (*δαιμόν*) serves as a guiding spirit, yet its darker expression as Threshold Guardian demands opposition, reflecting one's inner chaos in a form to be surmounted.

The daemonic double is not stagnant; it progresses with the practitioner's evolution, growing more subtle and multifarious as deeper layers of the self are uncovered. Its presence ensures that spiritual advancement is earned through direct engagement with one's own limits, making it a facilitator of transformation rather than mere obstacle.

As Dweller on the Threshold, the daemonic double fulfills a dual purpose: it hinders the unworthy, refining the resolute. It stands at the liminal boundary between profane and sacred, testing one's power to surpass attachment and illusion. Evola frames this encounter as an alchemical ordeal in *The Hermetic Tradition,* likening it to the *Nigredo* phase — the dark, chaotic precursor that must be purified into spiritual gold.

This trial is a recurring process, with each level presenting a new guardian as an initiate ascends through successive stages of awareness. The daemonic double serves as both adversary and teacher, compelling one to integrate fragmented aspects of the self into a unified, sovereign whole.

Ritual of Confrontation and Integration

This ritual offers a practical means to engage the Threshold Guardian. Intended for a realized spiritual presence, the process empowers one to face, dialogue with, and ultimately assimilate this entity, turning it from an obstruction into an ally.

Preparation

Conduct the ritual at midnight, when the veil thins. Fast for four hours prior to sharpen focus and receptivity. Bathe with sea salt and oil, then don a robe made of natural fibers.

Prepare a quiet, dimly lit room free of disruptions. Position the altar facing north and arranged with a black candle (the daemonic double), white candle (the higher self), mirror (for confrontation), bowl of water (reflection), and symbol of Hermes Trismegistus (psychopomp and guide).

Ritual Performance

Light the incense and candles, sanctifying the space. Stand before the altar, breathe deeply, and envision a radiant ring of protection encircling you. Recite:

Καθαρίζω τὸν χῶρον καὶ τὸν ἑαυτόν μου, ἵνα ἁγνὸς ᾖ πρὸς τὸ ἔργον τῆς μαγείας.

Katharízō tòn chō̃ron kaì tòn heautón mou, hína hagnòs êi pròs tò érgon tês mageías.

"I cleanse this space and myself, that I may be pure for the work of magic."

Raise your hands with palms upward and invoke Hermes Trismegistus, reciting:

Εἰς τὸν Ἑρμῆν τὸν Τρισμέγιστον, τὸν ὁδηγὸν τῆς σοφίας, κράζω. Ἔλθοι μοι, ὦ Ἑρμῆ, καὶ ὁδήγησόν με εἰς τὴν συνάντησιν τοῦ δαιμονικοῦ διπλοῦ.

Eis tòn Hermên tòn Trismégiston, tòn hodēgòn tês sophías, krázō. Élthoi moi, ō Hermê, kaì hodḗgēsón me eis tề̄n synántēsin toû daimonikoû diploû.

"To Hermes the Thrice-Greatest, guide of wisdom, I call. Come to me, O Hermes, and lead me to the encounter with the daemonic double."

Sit before the mirror, locking eyes with your reflection, and visualize the daemonic double rising from its depths. Address it firmly:

Ὦ δαιμόνιον διπλοῦν, φύλαξ τοῦ κατωφλίου, ἔρχομαι πρὸς σὲ μετὰ θάρρους καὶ σαφήνειας. Ἀποκάλυψον τὸ πρόσωπόν σου, ἵνα γνῶ σε καὶ ἑνωθῶ μετὰ σοῦ.

Ō daimónion diploûn, phýlax toû katōphlíou, érchomai pròs sè metà thárrous kaì saphēneías. Apokálypson tò prósōpón sou, hína gnō̂ se kaì henōthō̂ metà soû.

"O daemonic double, guardian of the threshold, I come to you with courage and clarity. Reveal your face, that I may know you and unite with you."

Observe its form, meeting its prominence with unwavering determination. Initiate a mental exchange, posing:

"What do you embody within me?"

"What lessons do you bear?"

"How may I weave your essence into my being?"

Receive its responses as thoughts, sensations, or visions, embracing its presence with acceptance rather than aversion. Envision the daemonic double merging with your higher self, the black and white candlelights fusing into a golden glow. Declare:

Ἐγὼ εἰμι τὸ φῶς καὶ τὸ σκότος, τὸ ἕν καὶ τὸ διπλοῦν. Ἐν τῇ ἑνώσει μου, εὑρίσκω τὴν ἀληθῆ δύναμιν.

Egṑ eimi tò phôs kaì tò skótos, tò hén kaì tò diploûn. En têi henṓsei mou, heurískō tḕn alēthê dýnamin.

"I am the light and the darkness, the one and the double. In my union, I find true power."

Sense its energy integrating, shifting from an external foe to inner potency. Offer gratitude, reciting:

Εὐχαριστῶ τῷ Ἑρμῇ διὰ τὴν ὁδηγίαν καὶ τὴν προστασίαν.

Eucharistô tôi Hermêi dià tḕn hodēgían kaì tḕn prostasían.

"I thank Hermes for his guidance and protection."

Extinguish the black candle, followed by the white, signifying completion. Ground yourself by drinking from the water cup.

Chronicle the encounter in a journal — its form, dialogue, and discoveries. Contemplate its impression on your self-insight and spiritual trajectory, applying this understanding through meditation and action.

The Trial of the Threshold is a crucible for spiritual sovereignty wherein the daemonic double tests and tempers an initiate. Through invocation and absorption, one transcends the fragmented self, aligning with the Hermetic pursuit of *Henosis* — achieving unity with god as higher self. This ritual provides a practical framework for a transformative encounter, furthering a realized spiritual life rooted in courage, clarity, and ascent.

Rubedo and Sovereignty

The pinnacle of transformation in the alchemical tradition is when one transcends the profane to attain deific awareness and spiritual dominion. This journey involves progressing from the Golden Magus associated with the *Citrinas* stage, to the Red King embodying *Rubedo* and attainment of the Philosopher's Stone. Grasping this state, it culminates in a ritual of consecration utilizing the traditional Hermetic working tools of wand, dagger, cup, and pentacle.

Rubedo marks a final phase of the Great Work in alchemy, where one achieves the Philosopher's Stone, signifying a final transmutation via integration with the godhead. Represented by the color red, *Rubedo* signifies an alchemical apex, embodying the state of spiritual sovereignty known as *Henosis*, or union with the One. *Rubedo* is a lived reality wherein the practitioner becomes a deified being — an avatar: divinity in flesh.

The alchemical journey progresses through four stages: *Nigredo* (blackening), *Albedo* (whitening), *Citrinas* (yellowing), and *Rubedo* (reddening). Each stage purifies and refines the practitioner's consciousness, with *Nigredo* dissolving the ego, *Albedo* purifying the soul, *Citrinas* illuminating the mind, and *Rubedo* incorporating one's self into the divine order.

The Golden Magus, corresponding with the *Citrinas* phase, embodies an archetype of Solar Logos: divine intellect radiating wisdom like sun emits rays. As a Hermetic-Alchemical adept, the Golden Magus has refined their soul through the adversity of *Nigredo* and cleansing of *Albedo*. This is like extracting the gold within — an inner light that illuminates a path to godhood. The Golden Magus channels the Solar Logos, becoming a conduit for divine presence; yet this is not the final stage.

Citrinas, while a significant attainment, remains anchored in individual consciousness, preparing one for further refinement into a Red King. The Golden Magus wields the Hermetic tools — wand (will), dagger (discernment), cup (receptivity), and pentacle (manifestation) — to refine their spiritual faculties, but must excel even this enlightened state to achieve *Rubedo's* absolute concord with the cosmos.

The Red King, embodying the *Rubedo* stage, completion of the alchemical work, and attainment of the Philosopher's Stone, is an emblem of inner clarification and metaphysical mastery. This marks an overwhelming shift in consciousness, where one transcends personal limitations to become fully amalgamated with the source of all. It is to achieve living apotheosis.

In Evolian terms, this is the realization of the Absolute Individual — a state of spiritual authority where one is attuned with god consciousness, realizing lasting, embodied *Henosis*. Evola writes in *Theory of the Absolute Individual*, "The Absolute Individual is not bound by the transient; he is the eternal center, the one who commands the forces of existence."

The Philosopher's Stone, represented by the red gem in the ritual below, enables a practitioner to transmute reality not for material benefit, but to uphold cosmic order and guide others toward awakening. The Red King embodies this power, standing as a sovereign figure who has completed the Great Work.

Evola's concept of an Absolute Individual describes a state beyond ego and materiality: pure, limitless existence wherein one incarnates the deiform. This is *Henosis*, a Platonic concept of union with the One, source of all being, as described in the *Corpus Hermeticum.* In alchemy the Philosopher's Stone is key to this state, integrating body, soul, and spirit into a whole.

Henosis, in this context, is not a fleeting mystical experience but a stable, enduring state of divine consciousness achieved through rigorous pursuit of the alchemical process. An Absolute Individual exists with total freedom and authority (their actions reflecting the divine will) and serves as a bridge between man and the universe, accomplishing the Hermetic ideal of becoming a co-creator with the Cosmic Lord.

Ritual of Consecration

Designed for those who have conquered the Golden Magus state through practice and insight, this operation is a sacred act marking their ascension to Red King. It employs wand, dagger, cup, and pentacle alongside a golden sun disk and red gem as central to its layered symbolism. The golden sun disk represents the Solar Logos, an illuminated intellect, while the red gemstone embodies the Philosopher's Stone and culmination of *Rubedo.*

Ensuring authenticity and spiritual resonance, this ritual is structured with multiple phases, principal gestures, and Greek invocations. Hasty consecration risks ego inflation and psycho-spiritual imbalance, so one must be certain of their readiness, having mastered the prior stages through disciplined effort.

The ritual is performed at dawn, connecting to the Hermetic association of sunrise with deific awakening. Bathe with sea salt and oil to purify body and aura, then don a white robe of natural fabric. Prepare a quiet, dimly lit room. A small north-facing altar is assembled with the following tools:

Wand: Represents the element of fire and the practitioner's will, channeling godly intent.

Dagger: Symbolizes air and discernment, cutting through illusion to reveal truth.

Cup: Signifies water and receptivity, holding the essence of divine wisdom.

Pentacle: Denotes earth and materiality, grounding spiritual energies in the physical.

Golden Disk: Embodies the Solar Logos, the radiant intellect of *Citrinas*.

Red Mineral: Represents *Rubedo's* apex as the Philosopher's Stone.

A bowl of purified water and receptacle for the frankincense complete the altar.

A journal and pen are kept nearby for post-ritual reflection. The practitioner fasts for four hours prior to enhance mental clarity and spiritual sensitivity.

Purification and Sanctification

Light the incense and white candle placed at each side of the golden disk, symbolizing an ignition of the Solar Logos. Sprinkle water from the cup around the altar, creating a sacred boundary, and recite in Greek:

Καθαρίζω τὸν χῶρον τοῦτον καὶ τὸν ἑαυτόν μου, ἵνα ἁγνὸς ἦ πρὸς τὸ ἔργον τῆς μαγείας

Katharízō tòn chō̃ron toûton kaì tòn heautón mou, hína hagnòs êi pròs tò érgon tês mageías.

"I cleanse this space and myself, that I may be pure for the work of magic."

With the wand in the right hand, approach the center of the room. Facing the altar, trace a circle in the air around one's self, turning clockwise and visualizing a golden barrier of protection. After, take three deep breaths, inhaling through the nose and exhaling through the mouth, grounding oneself in the present.

Invocation of Hermes Trismegistus

Standing before the altar, raise the wand toward the heavens, invoking *Hermes Trismegistus*, guide of alchemical mysteries. In Greek recite:

Ω Ἑρμῆ Τρισμέγιστε, φύλαξ τῆς σοφίας, ὁδηγὲ τῶν μυστηρίων, κράζω πρὸς σέ. Ἐλθέτω μοι καὶ φώτισον τὴν ὁδὸν πρὸς τὴν ἔρυθρον κυριαρχίαν

Ō Hermê Trismégiste, phýlax tês sophías, hodēgé tôn mystēríōn, krázō pròs sé. Elthétō moi kaì phṓtison tḕn hodòn pròs tḕn érythron kyriarchían.

"O Hermes Trismegistus, guardian of wisdom, guide of the mysteries, I call upon you. Come to me and illuminate the path to red sovereignty."

Visualize Hermes appearing as a radiant figure holding a Caduceus, his presence enveloping the space in golden light, symbolizing the Solar Logos. The wand is placed on the altar, its fiery energy now internalized.

Alignment with the Solar Logos

The practitioner holds the golden sun disk in both hands, raising it to the face and gazing into its reflective surface, seeing their visage merge with the holy light. They recite:

Ἐν τῷ φωτὶ τοῦ Ἡλίου εὑρίσκω τὸν Χρυσὸν Μάγον, τὸν ἄγγελον τῆς σοφίας

En tôi phōtì toû Hēlíou heurískō tòn Chrysòn Mágon, tòn ággelon tês sophías.

"In the light of the Sun I find the Golden Magus, the messenger of wisdom."

They visualize their consciousness expanding, filled with the radiant energy of the Solar Logos, their mind illuminated with divine clarity.

Cutting Through Illusion

The practitioner takes the dagger in their right hand, raising it to the east, and recites:

Δια τῆς λεπίδος τῆς ἀληθείας, ἀποκόπτω τὰς ψευδεῖς σκιάς

Dià tês lepídos tês alētheías, apokóptō tàs pseudéis skiás.

"With the blade of truth, I cut away the false shadows."

Make a cutting motion in the air, picturing the blade severing attachments to persona, fear, and delusion. Each cut releases a dark mist that dissolves into light, symbolizing a purification achieved in Albedo and the clarity of *Citrinas*. The dagger is restored to the altar, its work complete.

Receptivity to Divine Wisdom

The practitioner lifts the cup with both hands, holding it at heart level, and recites:

Ἐν τῷ ποτηρίῳ τῆς καρδίας, δέχομαι τὴν θείαν γνῶσιν

En tō potēriō tēs kardias, dechomai tēn theian gnōsin.

"In the cup of the heart, I receive divine knowledge."

Visualize the cup full with a luminous liquid, representing the wisdom of the Solar Logos. Take a sip of water from the cup, feeling divine insight permeate life, aligning one's actions with the True Will. The cup is placed back on the altar, its receptive energy integrated.

Manifestation of the Alchemical Work

The practitioner takes the pentacle, pressing it to their chest, and recites:

Δια τοῦ πενταγράμμου, στερεῶ τὴν ἔργον τῆς μεταμορφώσεως

Dià toû pentagrámmou, stereô tèn érgon tês metamorphṓseōs.

"Through the pentacle, I solidify the work of transformation."

Envisage a pentacle grounding their spiritual energies into the physical world, anchoring the illumination of *Citrinas*. The pentacle is replaced at the altar, its stability supporting the rise to *Rubedo*.

Transformation to Rubedo

Hold the red gem, symbol of the Philosopher's Stone, and raise it above the golden sun disk, visualizing the golden light of *Citrinas* deepening into a vibrant red glow. Recite:

Ἐκ τοῦ χρυσοῦ εἰς τὸ ἔρυθρον, ἐκ τῆς σοφίας εἰς τὴν κυριαρχίαν, μεταμορφοῦμαι

Ek toû chrysou eis tò érythron, ek tês sophías eis tèn kyriarchían, metamorphoûmai.

"From gold to red, from wisdom to sovereignty, I am transformed."

Feel consciousness shift, merging with the essence of the Stone and embodying the Red King's dominion. Grasp the gem firmly, its dynamism emanating through one's being.

Affirmation of Sovereignty

Standing tall, the practitioner raises both arms, holding the gemstone in their right hand and disk in the left, declaring:

Ἐγὼ εἰμι ὁ Βασιλεὺς Ἐρυθρός, κύριος τῆς Πέτρας τῶν Φιλοσόφων. Ἐν τῇ ἑνώσει μου μετὰ τοῦ θείου, εὑρίσκω τὴν ἀληθῆ κυριαρχίαν

Egò eimi ho Basileùs Erythròs, kýrios tês Pétras tôn Philósophōn. En têi henṓsei mou metà toû theíou, heurískō tèn alēthê kyriarchían.

"I am the Red King, lord of the Philosopher's Stone. In my union with the divine, I find true sovereignty."

They visualize themselves as a radiant figure cloaked in red, standing at the center of the cosmos, their will as one with the ultimate godhead.

Integration and Contemplation

The practitioner sits before their altar, placing the gem and disk side-by-side, and meditates silently for 8-12 minutes. They reflect on the journey from *Nigredo* to *Rubedo*, visualizing each stage — dissolution, purification, illumination, and completion — merging into a unified whole.

They recognize themselves as the Red King embodying the Philosopher's Stone, with the golden sun disk's light now fully integrated into their red aura, symbolizing *Henosis*.

Thanksgiving and Closing

The practitioner stands and recites a Prayer of Thanksgiving:

Εὐχαριστοῦμεν σοι, ὦ ἄρρητε ὄνομα, τὸ τιμώμενον ὡς θεός, τὸ αἰνούμενον ὡς πατήρ, ὅτι πᾶσιν καὶ πᾶσιν ἔδειξας πατρικὴν εὐσέβειαν, φιλίαν, ἀγάπην, καὶ γλυκυτάτην ἐνέργειαν, δωρούμενος ἡμῖν νοῦν, λόγον, γνῶσιν

Eucharistoûmen soi, ō árrēte ónoma, tò timṓmenon hōs theós, tò ainóumenon hōs patḕr, hóti pâsin kaì pâsin édeixas patrikḕn eusébeian, philían, agápen, kaì glukutátēn enérgeian, dōroúmenos hēmîn noûn, lógon, gnôsin.

"We give thanks to you, o ineffable Name, honored as God and praised as Father, for to everyone and everything you have shown fatherly kindness, affection, love, and sweetest activity, granting to us mind, word, and knowledge."

This prayer expresses gratitude for divine revelation, sealing the ritual's intent. The practitioner extinguishes the candle and incense, drinks from the cup to ground themselves, and places the tools reverently on the altar.

After the ritual, the practitioner journals their experiences, noting visions, sensations, or insights. They reflect on how the ritual has deepened their connection to the divine, considering how to integrate this sovereignty into daily life through ethical action, meditation, and study of Hermetic manuscripts like the *Corpus Hermeticum*. Annual practice of this consecration strengthens the practitioner's embodiment of the Red King.

The ritual is reserved for those who have mastered the Golden Magus state through prior spiritual work, as hasty recital risks egomania and psychic instability. Approach the ritual in a stable mental and emotional state, ensuring one has entirely completed training through meditation, practice, and study.

If distress arises, they should pause, ground themselves, and resume in a cautiously deliberate manner. The ritual should be performed in a private, quiet space to avoid interruptions, and one must approach it with reverence, aligning intent with spiritual transcendence rather than personal gain.

The wand, dagger, cup, and pentacle correspond to elements and faculties of the practitioner, mirroring the alchemical stages and facilitating a passage from *Citrinas* to *Rubedo*. As central symbols, the golden sun disk and red crystal symbolize the Solar Logos and Philosopher's Stone respectively, creating a lattice of significance that aids a practitioner's merger with deific being.

The Prayer of Thanksgiving is a historically attested Hermetic hymn found in the *Asclepius*, reflecting the operation's reliance upon established knowledge. The ritual's structure also incorporates traditional Indo-European components like Vedic meditation and the heroic ethos of ancient Greek philosophy, emphasizing self-mastery and Uranian vigor over sophisticated clerical adherences.

The journey from Golden Magus to Red King signifies the apex of alchemical transformation, attaining the Philosopher's Stone and embodying the Absolute Individual. The practitioner achieves lasting *Henosis*, personifying spiritual sovereignty.

With its layered symbolism and thorough steps, this ritual offers a practical induction for those who exceeded the *Citrinas* stage. It demands readiness and grave respect to avoid spiritual peril. By accomplishing this grade, one fulfills Evola's vision of surpassing the material province to become a deified being, ascending the spiritual heights of the cosmos and beyond.

The Absolute Individual in Society

The Absolute Individual represents the pinnacle of spiritual evolution — one who has outshined the limitations of modernity and personified Traditional principles. He is a sovereign being who has transcended societal constraints, embodying ageless actualities. As Baron Julius Evola articulates in *Theory of the Absolute Individual*, "The Absolute Individual is the one who has realized the divine within, becoming a law unto themselves."

This state is not a passive achievement. It is the result of rigorous spiritual discipline, rejecting the contaminated values of modern culture. The Absolute Individual serves as a bridge between spirituality and the mundane, upholding Tradition — a metaphysical order rooted in timeless understanding — amidst civilizational decay.

This concept draws heavily from Hermeticism, particularly the *Corpus Hermeticum*, wherein Hermes Trismegistus asserts "the universe is mental," suggesting inner transformation can influence reality. The Absolute Individual, having undertaken the Great Work (*Magnum Opus*) of alchemical magic, embodies this principle.

As described in Evola's *The Hermetic Tradition*, this process encompasses transmuting the soul, illuminating the mind, and incorporating the self with the divine, resulting in a being who stands as a beacon of spiritual authority.

The Absolute Individual participates in modernity while remaining separate from its materialism and decadence. Evola views contemporary society as a landscape of cultural decline characterized by consumerism, inversion, and crudeness. In *The Hermetic Tradition*, he urges a spiritual elite to stand against the modern world, preserving esoteric knowledge and guiding those capable of surpassing the conformist decay. This detachment is not seclusion, but an earnest refusal to follow corrupted norms and insincere beliefs, allowing the Absolute Individual to remain a custodian of Tradition.

As aristocrats of the soul, these individuals form a spiritual elite responsible for upholding an "invisible chain" of Tradition, as outlined in *Introduction to Magic*. Their role is not to reform society *en masse*, but inspire and guide genuine seekers toward awakening. This corresponds with the Hermetic principle of correspondence, wherein the alteration of individuals reflects and influences the greater organism. Through their examples and teachings, the spiritual elite offer a conduit out of societal decline, conveying ageless wisdom in a world that has generally disregarded it.

The charge of a metaphysical elite, or spiritual nobility, is to preserve Tradition amidst cultural and civilizational erosion. Evola emphasizes that Tradition is not a relic of the past but a living, metaphysical reality that must be actively upheld.

In *Theory of the Absolute Individual* he describes this elite as those who carry the flame of the divine in an age of darkness. This responsibility involves both safeguarding esoteric knowledge and transmitting it to those worthy of receiving, ensuring the sacred remains untainted by modern distortions.

This obligation is encumbered with challenges, as modernity threatens to destroy sacred ideals through secular materialism. The spiritual elite must therefore cultivate resilience, discipline, and discernment — qualities Evola associates with honorable, virile principles of ancient societies. By embodying these virtues, they serve as living archetypes of Tradition, countering the decay around them and fostering a nucleus of awakened individuals capable of perpetuating its legacy.

Hermetic principles postulate a convincing means of countering modernism by inspiring restitution and fostering awakening. The *Corpus Hermeticum* teaches reality is shaped by consciousness, a perception that corresponds with Evola's vision of reawakening the aristocrats of the soul to their divine potential. Arthur Versluis, in *The Philosophy of Magic*, argues that Hermeticism's focus on inner transformation can counteract the disenchantment of the modern world, restoring a sense of the sacred. By making these teachings accessible, one can promote a return to sanctified values.

However, Evola cautions against diluting esoteric knowledge for mass consumption. In *The Hermetic Tradition*, he insists the esoteric must remain veiled, accessible to those with authority, restraint, and the insight to wield it responsibly. This tension between preservation and accessibility is a central challenge for societal regeneration.

The spiritual elite must balance transmitting wisdom to genuine seekers while protecting it from trivialization, adhering to the Hermetic maxim "*to know, to will, to dare, to keep silent.*" Through this discerning approach, Hermetic principles can inspire a measured reawakening, laying the groundwork for a culture rooted in spiritual depth.

Hermeticism provides timeless insights for contemporary seekers pursuing the *Magnum Opus* — the alchemical process of metaphysical transformation. The *Greek Magical Papyri* and *Hermetica* outline practices such as meditation, invocation, and discipline to summon godly power. The UR Group's *Introduction to Magic* series offers concrete guidance, urging esotericists to become a living embodiment of Tradition.

This requires guiding students through direct transmission and example, awakening their inner potential rather than merely imparting knowledge. By integrating these Hermetic insights, seekers and teachers can achieve spiritual sovereignty and contribute to the preservation of Tradition in a modern context.

We support a *counter-occulture* based on a Northern Esoteric Tradition, rooted in Indo-European spirituality, and allied with Hyperborean ideals. This emphasizes virility, ascesis, and a return to primordial realism, drawing from sources like the *Greek Magical Papyri*, which utilize noticeably archaic elements. In *The Hermetic Tradition*, Evola explains our doctrines as the source of all true spirituality, return to a primordial center, and echo of a golden age.

This counter-occulture is not historical reenactment. It is a reconnection with sacred functions of Indo-European tradition including the heroism of ancient Greece, meditative disciplines of Vedic spirituality, and apotheosis of Egyptian pharaohs. By advancing an order allied with these ideals, a Northern Esoteric Tradition offers a virile replacement to present-day Occulture, promoting an upright, masculine expression of celestial order.

The Absolute Individual as envisioned by Evola stands as an archetype of transcendent anomie in a decaying world. Through detachment from modernity and orientation toward Tradition, this individual, together with a spiritual elite, upholds timeless wisdom and influences others toward transcendence. Hermetic principles provide a conduit for cultural restitution, balancing conservancy with availability while offering practical guidance for seekers pursuing the *Magnum Opus*.

The Northern Esoteric Tradition, rooted in Indo-European spirituality and Hyperborean ideals, emphasizes the need for a counter-occulture to restore vitality, order, and primordial truth. Together, these form a robust amalgam for resisting decline and fostering a spiritually awakened society.

The path of the Absolute Individual is a call to rise above the malaise of modernity and reclaim a divine potential within. In an era marked by cultural fragmentation and social uncertainty, a transcendent elite serve as beacons illuminating the way for those pursuing a higher path. Guided by the understanding of Hermes Trismegistus, a seeker has the power to transform oneself and by extension the world around them.

The Northern Esoteric Tradition calls for courage to stand apart, wisdom to discern the sacred, and strength to uphold Tradition. As Evola reminds us, the Absolute Individual is not merely a solitary figure but a catalyst for a new dawn, where the divine order is reflected in human action.

Let us, therefore, take up this sacred charge. Let us meditate daily on the divine *Nous*, invoke the guidance of ancient wisdom, and live with the integrity of a spiritual elite. In doing so, we weave a tapestry of renewal, restoring the sacred to a world in need. The journey is arduous, but the reward is nothing less than a realization of our godlike nature — an autonomy that echoes through eternity.

A profound truth reminds us that the path to the Absolute Individual is a journey toward unity with the divine. It is a light guiding us through the darkness of modernity to the eternal. As Hermes Trismegistus declares:

Εἰ οὖν μὴ ἴσος τῷ θεῷ γένῃ, οὐ δύνασαι καταλαβεῖν τὸν θεόν· ὅμοιον γὰρ ὁμοίῳ γινώσκεται.

Ei oún mí ísos tó theó géni, ou dýnasai katalaveín tón theón: ómoion gár omoío ginósketai.

"If then you do not make yourself equal to God, you cannot apprehend God; for like is known by like."

— Corpus Hermeticum, Book XI

www.ingramcontent.com/pod-product-compliance
Lightning Source LLC
LaVergne TN
LVHW010949110826
845149LV00015B/3270

* 9 7 8 1 9 6 8 3 9 4 0 4 2 *